Martin James Childs

1997

Good News for Everyone

£1-00

05/23

D0860613

Good News for Everyone

How to Use the Good News Bible
(Today's English Version)

EUGENE A. NIDA

Collins

FOUNT PAPERBACKS

First published in the United States of America in 1977
by Word Books, Publisher, Waco, Texas

First published in Great Britain in 1977 by Fount Paperbacks

All Scripture quotations, unless otherwise identified, are
from Today's English Version of the Bible. Copyright ©
American Bible Society 1966, 1971, 1976. Used by per-
mission. Scripture quotation from *Selections for New
Readers* is used by permission of the American Bible
Society. Scripture quotations from the Revised Standard
Version of the Bible, copyrighted 1946, 1952, © 1971, 1973
by the Division of Christian Education of the National
Council of the Churches of Christ in the U.S.A. and used
by permission.

Copyright © 1977 by Word, Incorporated, Waco, Texas 76703

Made and printed in Great Britain
by William Collins Sons & Co. Ltd, Glasgow

CONDITIONS OF SALE
This book is sold subject to the condition
that it shall not, by way of trade or otherwise,
be lent, re-sold, hired out or otherwise circulated
without the publisher's prior consent in any form of
binding or cover other than that in which it is
published and without a similar condition
including this condition being imposed
on the subsequent purchaser

Contents

Preface

It has been a distinct pleasure and privilege to know personally the team of translators who have prepared the *Good News Bible*. Most of these men have been my colleagues in the work of the United Bible Societies, and I have learned to appreciate not only their intellectual integrity but also their deep Christian convictions.

In the preparation of these notes on the committee's work, I have been especially helped by a series of insightful comments prepared by Dr. Roger Bullard and by the valuable assistance of my associates, Paul C. Clarke and Lucy Rowe.

As I have read through the text of this meaningful translation, I have become increasingly impressed with the solid scholarship of the translators and with their devotion to the principle of making accurate and faithful renderings which will make sense to the average reader. I trust, therefore, that the explanations of principles and procedures contained in this guide to the *Good News Bible* may do justice to the quality of their work and help the reader to understand what might otherwise be difficult to appreciate fully.

EUGENE A. NIDA

Greenwich, Connecticut
September 1976

Understood and Misunderstood

A translation of the New Testament selling more than 50,000,000 copies in less than ten years—a blind man attacked and robbed for distributing it—denounced by some people as the "masterpiece of the devil" yet praised by a newspaper editor as "the most readable of existing English translations"! All that is news. Most importantly it is Good News.

Both commended and condemned, understood and misunderstood, *Good News for Modern Man,* the New Testament title for Today's English Version, has simply experienced the treatment accorded almost all widely distributed translations. Three hundred and fifty years ago the translators of the King James Version were roundly denounced by many as having capitulated to the theological whims of their patron, King James the First of England. Some fifty years elapsed after its publication before this version was generally accepted by the English-speaking world. Such reactions to new translations of the Bible are typical because people so often resist change, especially in matters of religion. For many persons, to change the words of the Bible is tantamount to heresy. They do not realize that what is really changing is their own language and that, in order to preserve the meaning of the original message, the form of language must be altered from time to time so as to adjust the content of the message to the constantly changing forms of expression.

Even such a familiar passage as the opening verse of Psalm 1 in the King James Version can be quite misleading for many present-day readers: "Blessed is the man that walketh not in the counsel of the ungodly, nor standeth in the way of sinners, nor sitteth in the seat of the scornful." "Walketh not in the counsel" sounds to many persons today like "walketh not in the council," since in present-day English "to walk in the counsel of the ungodly" is not understood in the sense of "following the advice of ungodly persons." "Standeth in the way of sinners" seems equally strange, since to many people "to stand in the way of someone" can only mean "to block their path" or "to prevent them from going somewhere." And "to sit in the seat of the scornful" is a real puzzle. It can't, of course, have anything to do with musical chairs. If it means joining up with scornful people, what are these people scorning? This passage becomes so much clearer in the *Good News Bible:*

> "Happy are those
> who reject the advice of evil men,
> who do not follow the example of sinners
> or join those who have no use for God."

It is no wonder that one girl, after reading some of *Good News for Modern Man,* exclaimed, "Mommy, it must not be the Bible—I can understand it!"

The very fact that so many people have understood Today's English Version has no doubt caused a few people to misunderstand it. It was after the enthusiastic distribution of some 70,000 copies of *Good News for Modern Man* in the Concord and Kannapolis areas of North Carolina that one minister announced a Bible-burning ceremony. This turned into a "Bible burial" rally, with a mock funeral and a cross placed on the spot where the Today's English Version was interred. But in a letter to the editor, published in nearby newspapers, one teenager said, "I find that I can understand what I have read in *Good News* . . . instead of being confused." The editor himself wrote, "I would imagine a great percentage of the residents of this county do not understand the Bible and its terminology any more than we understand legal documents," and he concluded by speaking of Today's English Version as "the only thing that has come through in our lifetime to let us read and understand the Bible in our language."

Violence against Bible translators and distributors is nothing new in history. Tyndale, whose translation contributed so much to what later became the King James Version, was arrested, strangled, and burned at the stake for daring to render the message of God's Word into English. Before his day, the Lollards, who so effectively distributed Wycliffe's translation in England, were systematically persecuted, beaten, and often killed. Yet it does seem strange that in our day some people should have reacted so strongly against *Good News for Modern Man* that they would threaten to kill a blind man for distributing this message of salvation. That, however, is precisely what happened to Mr. J. C. Broom of Gulfport, Mississippi. After hurricane Camille struck that area in 1970, Mr. Broom began a special effort to distribute thousands of copies of the New Testament. Although he received some threatening phone calls, he continued his dedicated efforts to put the Scriptures into the hands of more and more people. Then one morning, when he answered a knock at his front door, he was attacked by a man with a knife. The man cut Broom's shirt, broke his cane, tied his hands to his feet, and put a pillowcase over his head. After scattering his stock of Scriptures, robbing him of what money he had, and mutilating some copies of the *Good News*, he departed with this warning: "You were told not to give away any more!" Later the same man phoned, saying, "Sooner or later we'll get you."

Most distributors of Today's English Version, however, have had much more pleasant experiences. One of them exclaimed: "Sharing the *Good News* there at the shopping plaza last Saturday has been one of the most rewarding experiences of my life. I would not have missed it for anything, especially when that lady returned to tell me, 'Those words are so wonderful.'"

One of the principal reasons why "those words are so wonderful" is that they are so understandable, for the translation is produced in what is known as "the common language." This is the kind of language common to both the professor and the janitor, the business executive and the gardener, the socialite and the waiter. It may also be described as "the overlap language" because it is that level of language which constitutes the overlapping of the literary level and the ordinary, day-today usage. The overlap area is itself a very important level, for it probably constitutes the form of language used by fully 75 percent of people more than 75 percent of the time. It is essentially the same level of language in which the New Testament was first written, the so-called koine Greek. The term *koine* itself means "common," and it was precisely this type of "common language" which the Gospel writers employed to communicate their unique and priceless message. They refused to load their urgent message with the elaborate style of the professional Greek rhetoricians, and, at the same time, they kept their writings free from the slangy vulgarisms of the street.

In producing a translation of the Bible into common language, the translators of the *Good News Bible* have, of course, employed a written, not a spoken style; but they have kept in mind the fact that far more people hear the Scriptures read than ever read them for themselves. Hence the translators have constantly tried to be alert to how the words would sound to listeners. They felt that they could not afford to fall into the kind of mistake that, for example, occurs in the Revised Standard Version, "prophesy with lyres" (1 Chron. 25:1), which to the average listener would sound like "prophesy with liars."

A common-language translation, however, is not one with an artificially restricted vocabulary such as that of the *Bible in Basic English*, which is restricted to a fundamental vocabulary of some 800 words, with the result that some unnatural and awkward phrases occur, for example: "sounding his praise in the sea-lands" for "praising him in the islands" (Isa. 42:12); "give ear in heaven your living-place" for "listen from your dwelling place in heaven" (1 Kings 8:43); "get knowledge with their hearts" for "understand in their hearts" (John 12:40); and "the position of sons to himself" for "adoption as sons" (Gal. 4:5). At the same time, because a common language translation is intended for people everywhere who use English, it must avoid regionalisms. Similarly, it must avoid slang, for slang is usually short-lived and often quite provincial. For example, the adulterous woman mentioned in Proverbs 7:12 could be described as "cruising the streets," but only those familiar with this current slang term for the activity of "streetwalkers" would understand.

In producing the *Good News Bible* in common language, the "first and central aim" (as stated in the principles adopted by the committee) has been accuracy, that is, faithfulness to the meaning found in the original Greek, Hebrew, and Aramaic texts of the Scriptures. To achieve such accuracy it is essential that the translation reflect the principle of "dynamic equivalence" in meaning, for only thus can the translation communicate faithfully the message of the original writing. The principle of dynamic equivalence is by no means a new one. It was, in fact, stated most effectively by Martin Luther when he said: "Whoever would speak German must not use Hebrew style. Rather, he must see to it—once he understands the Hebrew author—that he concentrates on the sense of the text, asking himself, Pray tell, what do the Germans say in such a situation? Once he has the German words to serve the purpose, let him drop the Hebrew words and express the meaning freely in the best German he knows."

The principle of dynamic equivalence implies that the quality of a translation is in proportion to the reader's unawareness that he is reading a translation at all. This principle means, furthermore, that the translation should stimulate in the new reader essentially the same reaction to the text as the original author wished to produce in his first and immediate readers. The application of this principle of dynamic equivalence leads to far greater faithfulness in translating, since accuracy in translation cannot be reckoned merely in terms of corresponding words but on the basis of what the new readers actually understand. Many traditional expressions in English translations of the Scriptures are either meaningless or misleading. How many present-day readers would know, for example, that "children of the bridechamber" (Matt. 9:15) really means "the guests at a wedding party" or that "bowels of mercies" (Col. 3:12) is better rendered as "compassion"?

In Today's English Version measures of cubic contents such as "bath," "hin," "homer," and "ephah" are expressed in terms of present-day equivalents, and the geographical term "Cush" is normally translated as "Sudan." The phrase

"Abraham's bosom" (Luke 16:22), especially misleading to the
average reader, actually refers to the heavenly feast of the
righteous. Thus the *Good News Bible* is both accurate and
meaningful in rendering the first part of Luke 16:22 as "The
poor man died and was carried by the angels to sit beside
Abraham at the feast in heaven." In some instances, however,
it is impossible to find a present-day equivalent of some
ancient objects or customs. The "Urim and Thummim" can
only be referred to as Hebrew borrowings, since scholars
simply do not know what these objects were. We know only
that they were employed in some way to determine the will of
God, and this is the explanation given for "Urim and Thummim" in the Word List of the *Good News Bible*.

The idea is sometimes held that a dynamic equivalent
rendering of the Scriptures is merely a paraphrase, rather
than a translation. However, Professor J. Ramsey Michaels,
Professor of New Testament and Early Christian Literature
at Gordon-Conwell Theological Seminary, writing in *Eternity*
magazine concerning Today's English Version, declared: "But
it is a real translation, in distinction from a paraphrase on the
one hand and mere word-for-word transposition on the other."
As a translation, the *Good News Bible* aims at the "closest
natural equivalence," and this may very well result in certain
significant changes in the formal arrangements of words. For
example, there is a well-known tendency in the Hebrew of
the Old Testament and in the Semitic-influenced Greek of
the New Testament to avoid direct mention of God. As a
consequence, a literal translation such as "Judge not that you
be not judged" (Matt. 7:1) leads most people to assume that
one should not criticize others in order not to be criticized in
turn. The context, however, indicates clearly that it is God
who does the judging. Hence, by taking into consideration
the Semitic tendency to avoid direct references to God by
means of passive constructions, the *Good News Bible* has rendered Matthew 7:1–2 as "Do not judge others, so that God
will not judge you—because God will judge you in the same
way you judge others, and he will apply to you the same rules
you apply to others."

In order to produce a faithful translation of the original text of Scripture, it may be necessary to replace some possibly misleading figures of speech by terms which are not figurative. "Lips" may often be more accurately rendered as "speech"; "God's strong arm" is better translated in some passages as "God's power," and "the horn of salvation" (Luke 1:69) is more faithfully rendered as "mighty Savior."

A comprehensible and accurate translation may also require the breaking up of some long, unwieldy sentences. Such sentences are natural enough in Greek or Hebrew, but they become impossible when reproduced literally in English. The first seven verses of the Letter to the Romans constitutes a single sentence in the original Greek—and this sentence does not even have a principal verb. This complex introduction to Paul's letter can only be made meaningful to the average reader in English if the long sentence is broken up into shorter expressions. Merely changing the punctuation of one of the traditional English translations would only obscure even more the connections of thought. To be a faithful rendering of the original message, its verbal form must be restructured to meet the grammatical requirements of the receptor language, English, while at the same time preserving the meaning of the original. Compare, for example, just the first three verses of this passage in the King James Version with its rendering in the *Good News Bible:*

King James Version	*Good News Bible*
1 Paul, a servant of Jesus Christ, called to be an apostle, separated unto the gospel of God,	1 From Paul, a servant of Christ Jesus and an apostle chosen and called by God to preach his Good News.
2 (Which he had promised afore by his prophets in the holy Scriptures,)	2 The Good News was promised long ago by God through his prophets, as written in the Holy Scriptures. 3 It is about his Son, our Lord Jesus Christ: as to his humanity, he was born a descendant of David:
3 Concerning his Son Jesus Christ our Lord, which was made of the seed of David according to the flesh;	

Though the text of the *Good News Bible* has a few more words, it is a much more accurate and faithful rendering of the meaning of the Greek text, showing more clearly the connections of thought within the highly compact Greek expression.

At times it may also be necessary to add a so-called "classifier" in order to make the translation clear to modern readers. This means, for example, that "myrrh" may be identified as a "drug" in Mark 15:23. It is even more important to indicate that the "Asia" mentioned in Acts 16:6 was a "province"; modern readers might easily think that the reference is to the modern continent of Asia.

Problems of pronoun reference are a constant source of difficulty in any translation, for it is entirely too easy to pass over some obscure reference and leave the reader completely in the dark. In Jeremiah 4:13 the prophet is speaking about "the enemy," but the Hebrew text merely says "he." In verse 18 of the same chapter the Hebrew has "you have brought this on yourself," but who is referred to by the pronoun "you" is not clear. Accordingly, the *Good News Bible* reads "Judah, you have brought this on yourself."

Accuracy in historical details is also essential in faithful translating. A curious problem which has interested historians for many years is found in 1 Samuel 6:4. It is true that a Hebrew term in this verse may be rendered as "hemorrhoids," but it is also highly probable that the reference is to "tumors." The plague which struck the Philistines so suddenly in one city after another was associated with mice or rats, and these rodents are known to be carriers of the fleas which transmit bubonic plague. One of the most conspicuous symptoms of this plague is the growth of tumors, especially under the arms. Accordingly, in place of the traditional "hemorrhoids," Today's English Version reads more accurately "tumors."

In trying to make sense to the modern reader, there is always the danger that the translation will become too up-to-date with the result that the significance of the original will be distorted or lost. In translating Deuteronomy 26:5 one might possibly speak of the "wandering Aramaean" as "a homeless refugee," thus making him like one of the millions of homeless people in the world today. But such a phrase would not accurately describe the Bedouin type of existence of the ancient patriarchs. The people traveled with their flocks and herds from one grassland to another, carrying all their possessions with them. Theirs was a nomadic way of life, and they could scarcely be called "refugees."

The modern equivalent of David's weapon mentioned in 1 Samuel 25:29 would be a slingshot, a Y-shaped stick with rubber bands drawn back to provide propulsion. But to translate the Hebrew term as "slingshot" rather than "sling" would be a clear anachronism, since rubber was not known in the ancient world. In reality, the ancient type of sling that was used by David had far more deadly force than any present-day slingshot.

In order to understand what a common-language and dynamic-equivalence translation really is, one should also realize what it is not. In the first place, it is not a translation made up simply of short sentences and simple words; this would make it seem childish. If a common-language translation is to live up to its name, it must be common to young and old alike, to the well-educated and to those with only limited education. However, a dynamic-equivalence translation must not be a "cultural translation," one which transposes the historical events of the original writers into another time-space context. *The Cotton Patch Version of the New Testament*, brilliantly produced by Clarence Jordan, represents precisely such a cultural transposition. It substitutes "Washington, D.C." for "Rome" and gives the name of "Rock Johnson" to "Cephas, son of John." But Today's English Version attempts no such time-space transpositions, for the historical context of the Scriptures is an integral part of the unique message of the Bible.

A dynamic-equivalence translation also avoids adding to the text explanations which are not implicit in the text itself. For example, to qualify "the Law" (John 1:17) with the phrase "with its rigid demands and merciless justice" (as in *The Living Bible*) is to introduce something quite foreign to either the text at this place or even the Scriptures as a whole.

In a sense a common-language translation is really quite

"uncommon" among translations. The fact that the *Good News Bible* is such a faithful and understandable translation of the Scriptures is only because of the dedicated efforts of many devout scholars. But this is another story, and it will be the theme of a later chapter.

CHAPTER TWO

Using and Understanding
the Good News Bible

Why does the Bible say that God called Eve "woman" because she came from man? Is the "City of David" the same in the New Testament as in the Old Testament? What are "mandrakes"? How does it happen that Hebrews 1:7 speaks of God making "his angels winds and his servants a flaming fire," while Psalm 104:4, the passage quoted in Hebrews, seems to say almost the opposite? Why do some translations of Ezekiel 8:17 speak of "putting the branch to their nose" while the *Good News Bible* reads "insults me in the most offensive way possible"?

These are the typical questions that the *Good News Bible* answers. The reader will find a wealth of information in the marginal notes, as well as in the indexes and special appendixes. This readable version thus becomes even more understandable.

For those ancient Hebrews who listened to the reading of the Scriptures, there was no difficulty in catching the play on proper names such as "Adam" and "Eve" (Gen. 3:20), for "Adam" in Hebrew also means "mankind," and "Eve" sounds very similar to the Hebrew word for "life," so that Eve could very well be thought of as the mother of "all human beings." Furthermore, they readily recognized how it was that Eve could be called "woman" since she was taken out of "man" (Gen. 2:23), for the Hebrew word *ish* means "man" and *isha* (basically the same root with a feminine ending) is the term for "woman." But for most English speakers all this subtle but highly significant information would be totally lost without some explanatory notes.

The number of proper names in the Bible with significant literal meanings is quite large, especially in the earlier chapters of Genesis, so that quite a number of marginal notes are necessary if the reader is to understand their meanings. Without them how will the ordinary reader know that Seth means "has given," Noah means "relief," Peleg "divide," Ishmael "God hears," Isaac "he laughs," etc.? In some instances there is more than one possible interpretation of a name. Beersheba may mean either "Well of the Vow" or "Well of Seven," and both meanings are significant (Gen. 21:31 and 26:33). The name Jacob also has two distinct meaningful connotations; it is related by popular etymology to "heel" (Gen. 25:26) and also to "cheat" (Gen. 27:36). Without an explanation of at least some of these important allusions to popular etymologies of proper names, the texts appear mystifying and even misleading.

In the Old Testament the phrase "City of David" refers to the Jebusite stronghold of Jerusalem, which was finally conquered during David's reign and made the capital of all Israel, but in the New Testament the same phrase refers to Bethlehem, the town where David was born and to which Joseph had to go to be registered, since he belonged to the lineage of David. A note in the Word List pointing out these facts may save a reader from being thoroughly confused.

From the context of Genesis 30:14 one would not know whether "mandrakes" were precious stones, animals of the field, mushrooms, or, in fact, almost anything! It is really important that the reader should understand that mandrakes were plants used as love charms, for their roots were believed to produce fertility. With a marginal note at this point in the text, Leah's reluctance to share her mandrakes with Rachel becomes quite understandable.

Some of the most perplexing difficulties in the Bible involve some of the quotations from the Old Testament made by New Testament writers. These men frequently quoted from the Greek Septuagint translation rather than making their own translation from the Hebrew text. This was a logical as well as a natural thing for them to do, since most of their readers would be much better acquainted with the Old Testament in the Greek translation than in the original Hebrew. As already mentioned, Hebrews 1:7 reads: "God makes his angels winds and his servants flames of fire," but the Hebrew text of Psalm 104:4, which obviously the writer is quoting, reads: "You use the winds as your messengers and flashes of lightning as your servants." If a reader compares these two verses, he is likely to be confused by the discrepancy unless he is told that the form employed by the New Testament writer is based on the Septuagint text rather than on the Hebrew. That is the reason why the *Good News Bible* has a list of all New Testament quotations made from the Septuagint when they differ significantly from the Hebrew. Some English translations have actually harmonized the Old Testament quotation to make it agree with the New Testament, but honesty and faithfulness to the Word of God demands that one refrain from altering the clear meaning of the original texts. Even a desire to bring harmony to what may otherwise seem to be an inexplicable discrepancy is no valid excuse for such tampering.

In some instances the *Good News Bible* renders an idiom by a nonidiomatic expression. The translation of a part of Ezekiel 8:17 reading "in the most offensive way possible" is explained in a marginal note as being "a reference to a pagan rite of putting a branch to the nose." Such a note makes it possible for the reader to understand why expressions used in other translations seem to be so different.

The supplementary helps in the *Good News Bible* are a veritable gold mine of indispensable information. For many readers, the most useful helps are the headings provided for the sections into which the text has been broken. These "section headings" do not attempt to explain the respective passages, but they are extremely useful in marking the beginning and end of important sections and in identifying their themes. This is often done by employing phrases which are simply lifted from the text itself. For example, "No One Knows the Day or Hour" is the section heading which identifies the contents of Mark 13:32–37. The headings for the various divisions in the Sermon on the Mount aid immensely in summarizing its contents, and the identifications of the speakers in the Song of Songs are crucial if one is to understand the abrupt shifts

in content. Unless the reader knows precisely when the words
are those of the man, the woman, or the accompanying chorus
of women, this otherwise beautiful poem can be a confusing
jumble. Moreover, the six different songs which comprise this
book are identified, and this also aids in comprehending the
breaks in the structure. Similarly, the identification of speakers
is also important in the book of Job, especially in chapter
27:13–23. Traditionally this section has been regarded as
being part of Job's words, despite the fact that its content is
so contrary to what Job has been saying all through the book.
It seems better, however, to suggest that these are more likely
the words of Zophar, since they are more in accord with what
Zophar has been saying. Similarly, for chapter 28 there is no
indication in the Hebrew text as to who the speaker is, and
this fact is important for the reader if he is to appreciate more
fully how this section fits in with what precedes and what
follows.

Along with the section headings there are the references
to parallel passages in other parts of the Bible. These "parallel
passage references" are especially important for the Gospel
records, but they can also be very useful in other places as
well, particularly in certain parts of the Old Testament. They
call attention to the fact that Psalms 14 and 53 are almost
identical and that Psalm 96 has a parallel in 1 Chronicles
16:23–33. Between the books of Kings and Chronicles there
are, of course, numerous parallel passages, and all of these
are conveniently marked by section headings and parallel
passage references.

Of all the various kinds of marginal notes, those which
explain alternative renderings are perhaps the most relevant.
An alternative rendering is simply another possible interpretation of a particular passage. There are almost a hundred
marginal notes giving alternative renderings in the New Testament of the *Good News Bible* and more than twice that many
in the Old Testament. One especially important alternative
rendering occurs in Genesis 28:14, which in the text reads:
"through you and your descendants I will bless all the nations";
but the Hebrew text here can also be interpreted as "all the
nations will ask me to bless them as I blessed you and your

descendants." Another interesting alternative interpretation occurs in Romans 3:9a, which is generally interpreted as, "Are we Jews in any better condition than the Gentiles? Not at all!" The same Greek text may, however, be understood to mean, "Are we Jews in any worse condition than the Gentiles? Not altogether."

Differences of texts and the corresponding marginal notes will be discussed in chapter 9. These should all be carefully noted by the reader, for they are important in understanding why various translations at times differ so much one from the other. If a reader finds the information in the *Good News Bible* insufficient to explain any New Testament textual difficulty, further important data can be obtained from the Greek New Testament published by the United Bible Societies and from a companion volume of the Greek text edited by Professor Bruce M. Metzger on behalf of the Greek New Testament Committee. (This volume is published by the United Bible Societies under the title of *A Textual Commentary on the Greek New Testament.*) Dr. Metzger's book contains a brief discussion of all the textual variants noted in the Greek New Testament and states the reasons for the committee's choice of one or another of the existing variants in various sets of manuscripts. A similar set of notes is being prepared at the present time to supply information concerning the various textual problems of the Old Testament.

Also important for the reader are notes which supply something of the historical background to statements at various points in the text. In Acts 12 it is important to identify King Herod as being Herod Agrippa I, who was the ruler of all Israel, for he needs to be distinguished from the three other Herods mentioned in the New Testament: Herod the Great, Herod Antipas, and Herod Agrippa II. Fortunately, all of these Herods, together with page references, are duly listed in the Index. It is also important to have a note on "Freedmen" in Acts 6:9, for the phrase "synagogue of Freedmen" seems rather strange without the explanation that "these were Jews who had been slaves, but had bought or been given their freedom." At times a phrase which has special historical relevance is not clear in its literal form or immediate context. In Romans

9:8 the Greek text, speaking of Abraham's descendants, reads more or less literally "this means that it is not the children of the flesh who are the children of God." In the *Good News Bible* the expression "children of the flesh" is rendered as "children born in the usual way," but even this phrase is obscure without a marginal note to explain that it "refers to the descendants which Abraham had through Ishmael, his son by Hagar (see Gal. 4:22–23)."

Perhaps even more important than the historical notes are those which explain differences in customs. In Genesis 24:2 the insistence of Abraham that his servant make a vow by placing his hand between Abraham's thighs would seem even more strange than it does if it were not for the explanation that "this was a way in which a vow was made absolutely unchangeable." In Exodus 29:37 it is important to have a note explaining the phrase "harmed by the power of its holiness," since otherwise the reader might not be aware of the ancient belief that ordinary people and things could be harmed by touching something which had been consecrated exclusively for the worship of the Lord.

Many of the more valuable notes concerning customs and cultural objects are to be found in the Word List, which, for example, identifies Asherah as "a goddess of fertility worshiped by the Canaanites; her male counterpart was Baal. After the Hebrews invaded Canaan, many of them began worshiping these two gods." There is likewise a helpful note concerning the "Festival of Dedication," which is described as "the Jewish festival, lasting eight days, which celebrated the restoration and rededication in 165 B.C. of the Temple altar by the Jewish patriot Judas Maccabeus. The festival began on the 25th day of the month of Kislev (around December 10). The Jewish name for this festival is Hannukah."

A particularly important explanation is given for the use of the term "outcasts" in the New Testament: "In the Gospels this name, which in many translations appears as 'sinners,' refers to those Jews who had been excluded from synagogue worship because they violated rules about foods that should not be eaten and about associating with people who were not Jews. Such outcasts were despised by their fellow Jews, and

Jesus was criticized for associating with them (Mark 2:15–17; Luke 7:34; 15:1–2)." Such notes as these provide the kind of supplementary information that is necessary for the Scriptures to speak meaningfully to the average reader.

The brief introductions to the various books are also a major aid to the reader. They are designed primarily to call attention to the major theme or themes of each book and to point out its major divisions. They can also be valuable in helping people to understand that the Bible is really not a single book, but a library containing different kinds of literature and many contrasting themes. Note, for example, the introduction to the Song of Songs:

> The *Song of Songs* is a collection of love poems, for the most part in the form of songs addressed by a man to a woman, and by the woman to the man. In some translations, the book is called *The Song of Solomon*, because it is attributed to Solomon in the Hebrew title.
>
> These songs have often been interpreted by Jews as a picture of the relationship between God and his people, and by Christians as a picture of the relationship between Christ and the Church.

Even such a brief introduction provides certain indispensable help to the reader who might otherwise be disturbed or puzzled by the presence of such a book in the Old Testament. Or note the introduction to an even more unusual Old Testament book, namely, Ecclesiastes:

> The book of *Ecclesiastes* contains the thoughts of "the Philosopher," a man who reflected deeply on how short and contradictory human life is, with its mysterious injustices and frustrations, and concluded that "life is useless." He could not understand the ways of God, who controls human destiny. Yet, in spite of this, he advised people to work hard and to enjoy the gifts of God as much as and as long as they could.
>
> Many of the Philosopher's thoughts appear negative and even depressing. But the fact that this book is in the Bible shows that biblical faith is broad enough to take into account such pessimism and doubt. Many have taken comfort in see-

ing themselves in the mirror of *Ecclesiastes*, and have discovered that the same Bible which reflects these thoughts
also offers the hope in God that gives life its greater meaning.

Such introductions can never be a commentary on the text—
they are not designed to be that—but they can point the
reader in the right direction so that in reading the book he
can have some understanding of its thrust and purpose.

The Word List, which has already been referred to in con-
nection with certain notes about customs and cultural objects,
is in some respects a miniature biblical encyclopedia, with
brief explanations about such varied words as Abib, Alabaster,
Areopagus, Beelzebul, Cumin, Dragon, Epicureans, Leviathan,
Nazirite, Purim, Snuffer, Zeus, and Ziv. The explanation of
the biblical meaning of "concubine" is especially useful, since
some persons suppose that the concubines of ancient times
were like the "mistresses" or "call girls" of today. The Word
List makes it clear, however, that a concubine was "a servant
woman who, although not a wife, had sexual relations with
her master. She had important legal rights, and her master was
referred to as her husband."

In addition to the various types of notes and helps printed
on the page with the text and in the Word List, there is also
a useful chronological table. Many of the dates given in this
table are of necessity only approximations. However, the list
of the succession of kings in Judah and Israel on the second
page of the chart is particularly valuable, especially since it
also notes the approximate periods in which various Old Testament prophets proclaimed their messages. There are also notes
concerning significant historical events which took place between the close of the Old Testament, toward the end of the
5th century B.C., and the beginning of the New Testament
accounts, starting with the announcement of the births of John
the Baptist and Jesus Christ, and ending with the final im-
prisonment of Paul, about A.D. 65.

The Index to the *Good News Bible* is different from most
Bible indexes in that it refers to a topic by page and not by
book, chapter, and verse. This means much more rapid "look-
up" for the average user and proves especially valuable for

Bible students who want useful lists of data on highly important themes or topics. The Index listing on "Abraham," for example, is essentially a brief summary of his life, calling attention to fifteen important events, in addition to providing important references to Abraham in the New Testament. The outline under "Angels" includes (a) messengers and agents of God, (b) angels in heaven, (c) angel of the Lord, (d) guardian angels, (e) guiding angels, (f) destroying angels, (g) the devil and his angels, and (h) angels with special individual names, such as Gabriel and Michael. Under "James" are listed the seven different persons in the New Testament who bear that name. Similarly, the Index distinguishes the seven persons named "Joseph," the six persons with the name of "Judas," the five women who were called "Mary," and the nine men known as "Simon."

Under "Miracles" are listed all the miracles of Jesus, as well as those performed by other persons, for example, Moses, Joshua, Samuel, Elijah, the apostles, Philip, Peter, and Paul. Under "Parables" are listed all those uttered by Jesus and also a number of parables which occur in the Old Testament.

In addition to persons and events, there are helpful indexes to the location of such major themes as Covenant, Covetousness, Divorce, Faith, Fasting, Forgiveness, the Holy Spirit, Judgment, Obedience, Peace, and Prayer. None of these themes can be treated in anything like a comprehensive manner, but the Index will at least introduce the reader to those places in the Bible where the crucial aspects of such themes are treated.

Twelve historical maps, reflecting some of the most recent archaeological discoveries in Bible lands, were especially prepared for the *Good News Bible*. These are grouped together in a map section in the back of the book together with a useful map index by means of which hundreds of towns, cities, rivers, lakes, mountains, and other geographical features mentioned in the Bible can be readily located in the maps. Since it is inconvenient for the reader to turn to the back of the book every time he wants to consult a map, most of these maps are repeated at convenient places throughout the text.

Yet another valuable feature of the *Good News Bible* is the series of illustrations prepared by Miss Annie Vallotton. These are so important as a means of drawing the reader to the text that they deserve to have their story told in detail. Chapter 3 in its entirety will be devoted to that theme.

It may seem strange to some readers that in a publication of the Bible Societies there should be so many helps for the reader in the form of marginal notes, indexes, section headings, reference systems, etc., when throughout the history of these societies so much emphasis has been placed upon publishing the Holy Scriptures "without note or comment." When that phrase was first used, and in fact throughout the entire history of its use, "without note or comment" has referred strictly to "dogmatic or doctrinal note or comment," notes which attempt to explain theological points of view or to argue particular interpretations. Right from the beginning the Societies have published Bibles with alternative readings (differences in textual evidence), and alternative renderings (differences in the interpretation of texts), explanations of plays on words, section headings (though usually gathered together as "chapter summaries"), maps, chronological indications, and indexes in the form of limited concordances. What seems to be new is the addition of noncontroversial notes concerning historical events and cultural features which are essential to the meaning of the text. Through the years the Bible Societies have been publishing such helps along with translations made in languages of the so-called Third World. There has usually been such a scarcity of books on biblical backgrounds in those languages that the addition of such supplementary helps was practically mandatory.

At a time when knowledge of biblical backgrounds was apparently far more widespread than it is today, the omission of such notes in English editions of the Scriptures might have been justified, but that is no longer the case. Similarly, there is an ever-increasing demand for some brief statement of the theme and contents of the various books of the Bible, not as substitutes for or explanations of the content, but as an aid to leading people to the text, with the hope that the text of Scriptures may thus speak more meaningfully, accurately, and effectively to those who wish to find the way to God in the Word of God.

CHAPTER THREE

Illustrations Which Illumine

Those pictures are incredible!

Where did the artist get the inspiration?

How can the artist say so much with so few lines?

These are only a few of the typical comments about the *Good News Bible* illustrations produced by Annie Vallotton, the dynamic Swiss artist whose rare skills and spiritual insights have combined to produce such an intriguing series of Bible illustrations.

While still a small child, Annie Vallotton showed unusual artistic abilities, and accordingly she was encouraged by her parents to study art. This she did with eagerness, including the classical and modern art of the Western world, the ancient art of Egypt, Babylonia, and Greece, Japanese woodcuts, and Eskimo sculpture. Finally, she settled upon line drawing as her preferred technique in illustrating books, especially books written for children. However, Annie Vallotton is by no means limited to a single artistic style. Her fabulous real-life sketches of Paris during the Nazi occupation are a tribute to her unusual skill in capturing both the moods and movements of people. Her documentary drawings of archaeological objects are remarkable for their accuracy of detail. But it is in her line drawings that she has achieved a singular capacity to say a great deal with only a few lines.

Annie Vallotton has various other skills, too. She is an accomplished song writer, and her captivating melodies seem to echo the musical motifs of Negro spirituals in speaking to the heart. She is a gifted speaker with contagious enthusiasm and a television artist amazingly adroit in illustrating a subtle point by means of a uniquely original drawing.

The illustrations which she prepared for *Good News for Modern Man* have proven so popular that they have not only been cited as outstanding examples of illustrative techniques, but have also been copied and reproduced in scores of ways: on greeting cards, tapestries, homemade quilts, wood carvings, and even cake decorations. But Annie Vallotton's drawings are not mere decorative devices, such as those which are found in so many medieval manuscripts, and much less are they designs for so-called "arty Bibles." Their purpose is not to embellish the pages nor to take the place of the biblical account, but to draw the reader to the text.

The drawings in the *Good News Bible* are purposely not historical and archaeological, for this would give the impression that the Bible is only a museum piece from the past and not a living book for the world of today. But neither are they based on present-day correspondences such as would be, for example, an illustration of a church bazaar as the equivalent of buying and selling in the Temple. The persons and scenes do in fact fit the historical setting of the Scriptures, but the near universality of movements, gestures, and background details makes them effective triggers for thought and windows for inspiration.

The real power in the Vallotton drawings rests in the depth of spiritual insight, so well illustrated by the manner in which the theme of Romans 6:6, "so that we should no longer be slaves of sin," is graphically marked by burdens being placed at the foot of the cross.

So that we should no longer be slaves of sin.

Again, note the way in which the contrast between "love" and "hate" is symbolized for 1 John 2:10-11. By gesture, facial expression, as well as by the background symbolization of light, the reality of these contrasting emotions becomes vividly portrayed:

He who loves his brother . . . he who hates his brother.

Or compare the contrast between the alms-giving showoff and the needy man (Matt. 6:2). Just enough background is shown to indicate that the ostentatious giving of a single coin was only to impress onlookers.

"Do not make a big show of it."

The key to the effectiveness of these illustrations is to be found in Annie Vallotton herself. She combines deep spiritual sensitivity, creative imagination, and technical competence in her own person. Even though her drawings for the New Testament had proven very popular, when plans were made for the entire Bible, the question arose as to whether it might be better to consider the style of some other artist. In order to find an answer the American Bible Society conducted a poll of its constituency through its magazine, the *Bible Society Record*. Three different types of illustrations were presented, and the readers were invited to express their preferences. The response was overwhelming in favor of the drawings of Annie Vallotton.

Annie Vallotton has a unique capacity to capture the significance of an event by portraying the movements and postures of participants. The rejection of idolatry is effectively dramatized for Deuteronomy 13:8 by having an earnest idolator offer a helpless, pathetic looking idol to a man who rejects it with both strength and determination.

"Do not even listen to him."

Emotions of joy and sorrow are strikingly portrayed by illustrations which are alive with movement. The dancing and singing of the Israelites (2 Sam. 6:5) is almost contagious and in such·vivid contrast to the slow-moving cart carrying the Covenant Box.

The Israelites were dancing and singing.

But note how different is the portrayal of King David's sorrow (2 Sam. 15:30) in which the olive trees themselves seem to be contorted in grief.

David went on up to the Mount of Olives, crying.

Emotions are often indicated merely by the position of the body, as in the case of Job 7:16 and 13:13.

"I give up; I am tired of living."

"Be quiet and give me a chance to speak."

And note how self-assured Job's counselors are, in contrast with Job himself (Job 16:1).

"The comfort you give is only torment."

One of the secrets of the Vallotton illustrations is the severe selectivity of features; everything which is not completely essential to the event is eliminated. For Matthew 15:14 the very absence of background and facial expressions communicates something about the blindness of the subjects.

"They are blind leaders of the blind."

On the other hand, facial features combined with posture are often strikingly employed to suggest emotions, as in Leviticus 19:17, Luke 12:22, and 2 Samuel 19:4.

"Do not bear a grudge."

"O my son! My son Absalom!"

So I tell you not to worry.

Another important element in the Vallotton illustrations is the exaggeration of focal features. The contrast between the pompous rich man and the poor, humble widow is portrayed by the exaggerated strutting of the foreground figure and the bare outline of the widow (Mark 12:41–44).*

A poor widow came along.

This same type of exaggeration of relevant details occurs in the illustration for Ecclesiastes 2, in which the king's large "bay window," the number of his female servants, and the

---

*This illustration appears in the paperback edition of *Good News for Modern Man* (Today's English Version of the New Testament). It is not included in the *Good News Bible*.

variety of their gifts all suggest idle luxury and conspicuous consumption, while the dog in the foreground is the very essence of boredom.

In the depiction of ancient events Annie Vallotton often employs the artistic styles typical of particular countries and periods. Note, for example, the typically Egyptian manner of representing the eyes of Pharaoh's daughter peering through the reeds (Exod. 2:5), while in the case of Sennacherib's attack upon fortified cities (2 Kings 18:13) Assyrian art forms are imitated.

The king's daughter noticed the basket.

Sennacherib attacked the fortified cities.

Annie Vallotton always takes great pleasure in depicting animals and children. Her animals always seem so much alive and her children so innocent and inquiring. The split picture of Genesis 7:8 is characteristic.

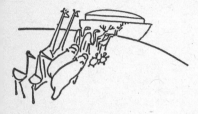

Every kind of animal and bird went into the boat.

For Psalm 71 the children not only symbolize the contrast between childhood and old age, but their sympathetic and inquiring attention makes the old man's declaration of praise to God so much more relevant.

No doubt part of the appeal of the Vallotton illustrations is the fact that they are completely different from what one is accustomed to. Who else would have thought of illustrating Nehemiah 13:17 by a man tramping out wine and others on their way to market?

"You're making the Sabbath unholy."

When artists make pictures of Zacchaeus, they usually put him up a tree, but Annie Vallotton illustrates this man's real problem, his small stature, by showing him almost lost in the crowd. Furthermore, by not picturing Jesus, she symbolizes Zacchaeus's plight in not being able to see what is happening.

He was a little man.

One of the most effective drawings depicts the "heroes of the wine bottle" (Isa. 5:22), in which drunkenness and despair are clearly written on the face of a man seen through a bottle.

Heroes of the wine bottle!

Though many of the pictures in the Vallotton series are without background, a number of them contain just enough lines to provide a setting, to illustrate a parallel happening, or to provide contrast. In the case of Isaiah 1:5 ("Israel, your head is already covered with wounds") the meaning of the figurative utterance is clearly indicated by the ruins of the city in the background.

Israel, your head is already covered with wounds.

For Jeremiah 14:3 the expression "they came back with their jars empty" is depicted by the foreground figure of the weeping woman and the jar turned down and strongly reinforced by the plight of the woman in the background who is trying so hard to reach down for water in a well which even lacks a rope.

They come back with their jars empty.

By reducing details as much as possible and by depicting emotions and attitudes primarily through gestures, postures, and body movements, Annie Vallotton has been able to provide a series of illustrations which are probably as universal in intelligibility as could possibly be produced. For Matthew 23:4 it is perfectly clear that the self-righteous onlooker is not willing to lift a finger to help those who are burdened with the loads of religious ritual and observances.

"They aren't willing even to lift a finger to help them."

And for 2. Corinthians 1:4 there is no difficulty in seeing how one man has come to "help those who have all kinds of troubles."

Help those who have all kinds of troubles.

Many of Annie Vallotton's illustrations appear to be so simple that one might wrongly assume that almost anyone could produce them, but that is far·from being the case. First, there must be both an intimate acquaintance with the Scriptures and a capacity to see beyond the mere words of the real life situations which they reflect. Then comes the process of making sketches—often a score or more before just the right one is produced. This is followed by consultation with specialists in biblical history, theology, and archaeology, so as to make certain that the illustration contains no anachronistic or discordant elements. All these things before the final drawing is made. Miss Vallotton produced at least twice as many drawings for the *Good News Bible* as have been used. Only those have been chosen which are most relevant to the reader and which fit satisfactorily within the format of the book.

Of all the recently published translations of the Bible, Today's English Version is the only one to come out with illustrations. This is no gimmick to increase sales. These pictures have been added so that the Word of life may come alive for the reader. By identifying in some measure with the drawings, he may also identify with the text and find in it the new kind of life made possible through the power of God as revealed in Jesus Christ.

CHAPTER FOUR

How It All Happened

The story of the *Good News Bible* begins not in the United States—nor even with the English language. It begins with Spanish Latin America. Some twenty years ago explorations in new approaches to Bible translating had produced amazing results. A Spanish translation in a *Versión Popular* was first prepared for the more than 10,000,000 Indians who live in Latin America all the way from northern Mexico to southern Chile. Many of them have a very limited knowledge of the Spanish language, and they needed the Scriptures in a version of Spanish that would be within the limits of their comprehension. To produce such a translation a number of scientific principles of communication were developed. (These were later explained in a highly useful volume written by Dr. William L. Wonderly, *Bible Translations for Popular Use*.) It was soon discovered that translations of portions of Scripture made in this *Versión Popular* were even more popular in places like Mexico City, Bogotá, and Buenos Aires than they were among Indians. The reasons for this were soon clear, for what had been produced was not a patronizing, stripped-down version of the Scriptures, but one which used the common language of the vast majority of Spanish-speaking people. Since this version avoided both the rhetorical elaboration of literary style as well as substandard slang and jargon, its use became increasingly widespread. When the entire New Testament appeared in print, it soon became a best-seller paperback.

A further stimulus for doing something similar in English

came from the creative work of a missionary in Liberia, Miss
Annie Cressman, whose translation of the New Testament into
the form of English used in West Africa showed how significant and important it would be to have a translation in a
more broadly based form of common English.

Having seen what could be done in Latin American Spanish
and in Liberian English, the American Bible Society decided
to undertake the preparation of Today's English Version of the
New Testament. The best person who could be found to undertake such work was Dr. Robert G. Bratcher, who, as a missionary in Brazil under the Southern Baptist Mission Board,
had had very valuable experience as a member of a committee to produce a revision of the famous d'Almeida Portuguese
version of the Bible. He had also taught Greek for a number
of years after completing his doctorate in New Testament
studies at Southern Baptist Seminary in Louisville, Kentucky.
Dr. Bratcher, who had only recently joined the Bible Society
staff, began at once to produce a kind of pilot translation of
the Epistle to the Ephesians. The first meeting on Today's
English Version took place in a Sunday school room of the
Madison Avenue Baptist Church in New York City. With
blackboard, chalk, copies of the text, some commentaries, and
a good supply of coffee, the members of the Translations Department of the Bible Society spent an entire day discussing
basic principles and procedures for doing in English what had
already been worked out over a number of years in Spanish.

The major responsibility for the text of *Good News for
Modern Man* fell to Dr. Bratcher, but various members of the
Translations Department and the Translations Committee of
the American Bible Society (especially Professor Howard Kee,
then of Drew Theological Seminary) also made important con-
tributions to the work.

The first sample text to be published was the Gospel of
Mark. This was such an immediate success that an all-out
effort was made to produce the entire New Testament as soon
as possible. A translation of the entire New Testament cannot
be made overnight, however, nor even in a year, because there
are so many problems—both large and small—which have to
be resolved. How, for example, is one to deal with biblical

terms for money? A Greek denarius contained only about twenty-five cents worth of silver, yet it was a day's wage for a common laborer. And how could one use the traditional term "talent," which in Greek refers to money? A silver talent was equivalent to some six thousand denarii and would have the buying power of at least ten thousand dollars in present-day values.

Moreover, the question of money equivalents was only one of the almost innumerable problems facing a translator. Far more difficult was the task of determining precisely what was the common-language level of English. Lists of word frequencies based on usage in books and newspapers were consulted, but they proved to be very inadequate guides. Some words are used rather infrequently, and yet they are known by almost everyone who speaks English. Furthermore, there are often no possible substitutes for some of these terms. The term "knee," for example, is low on the frequency list, but it must be used in translating. One certainly could not manufacture a substitute phrase such as "the bend in the middle of one's leg."

There are various editions of the Greek text in existence, and what Greek text to follow might have been yet another problem, but fortunately the United Bible Societies was just at that time completing a strategic ten-year program for the preparation of a new text of the Greek New Testament, edited by an international committee and designed especially to help translators.

Finally, on September 15, 1966, *Good News for Modern Man* was published in paperback form with a cover which reproduced the mastheads of leading newspapers throughout the world: the *Manila Times,* the *East African Standard,* the *Sydney Morning Herald,* the *Japan Times,* and the *New York Times.*

At the outset it was thought there would be only a limited demand for this new version. Accordingly, the American Bible Society decided to subsidize the publication to encourage its distribution, making it available for twenty-five cents a copy. But soon thousands of copies were being shipped from the warehouse every day, and the Bible Society was not able to continue the large subsidies which were required. The price was then increased to cover the actual cost of printing and mailing (without any addition, however, for translating, composition, and overhead costs); but the demand for copies continued to soar, and within six months more than two million had been sold. Within three years the total distribution had reached twelve million copies, not counting some forty million copies of individual books and selections. Before long *Good News for Modern Man* had surpassed all records in paperback sales, including Dr. Spock's *Baby and Child Care* and Jacqueline Susann's *Valley of the Dolls*.

Almost immediately, numerous requests for the entire Bible began to come to the Bible Society. Why stop with the New Testament, when, in many respects, the traditional language of most Old Testament translations is even more difficult for the average person to understand? But an Old Testament in common language could not be produced in two or three months, nor even in two or three years. The Old Testament is fully three times as long as the New Testament, and the problems of translation connected with it are so much more complex, especially because of the great differences in literary forms: historical narrative, lyric poetry, didactic sayings, prophetic utterances, legal codes, and others. Furthermore, a committee would be needed to carry out this task if it was to be finished in any reasonable period of time. But in September 1967, just one year after the publication of the New Testament, work began on the Old Testament. It was work which would require several years to complete.

The Old Testament Committee as finally constituted (some members joined at later stages in the work) consisted of seven men, all of whom had doctorates in biblical studies. In addition, all but one of them had served abroad as missionaries and so had had practical experience in translating into other languages. These men were uniquely equipped to appreciate the problems of communication and especially the need for making sense of difficult biblical expressions. They had had to wrestle with precisely such problems in trying to communicate the Good News in other languages.

Dr. Bratcher, as chairman of the committee, provided exceptional leadership. His rare combination of wit, scholarship, and personal devotion to the cause of Christ was the directive catalyst in the committee's work. Dr. Roger A. Bullard, a professor of New Testament Greek at Atlantic Christian College and a specialist in early Coptic Christian documents, showed particular skill in translating the so-called wisdom literature, but with the members of the committee he was perhaps most famous for his cartoons, which illustrated so effectively some of the humorous aspects of committee discussions.

Dr. Keith R. Crim, a former missionary in Korea who also had wide experience in editing, translating, and teaching, as well as being the author of a book of limericks, joined the team somewhat later than the rest, but he made up for lost time by his enthusiasm and concern for Hebrew poetic structures. Even in some of the most tedious and unlikely passages Dr. Crim rarely overlooked a possible pun.

Dr. Herbert G. Grether, formerly a missionary in Thailand and with many years of experience in preparing a new translation of the Bible into the Thai language, joined the committee after the work was well advanced. His deliberate, thoughtful, and kindly approach was very important in discussion. In spite of his generally mild manner, he did not give in readily if the issue under discussion was an important one.

Dr. Barclay M. Newman was known as the "commuting member" of the committee. He attended its major meetings while still carrying on his important work as a Translations Consultant of the United Bible Societies in Southeast Asia, where he has special responsibilities for the Malay and Indonesian languages and for a number of so-called "tribal tongues" of Eastern Malaysia. Dr. Newman not only provided keen scholarly insights but also a contagious sense of humor, though never at the expense of anyone else.

Dr. Heber F. Peacock likewise carried on his work with the Old Testament Committee while also serving as Translations Coordinator for Africa on behalf of the United Bible Societies. For a number of years he had been a teacher of Hebrew and Old Testament in various schools (Baptist Seminary in Rüschlikon, Switzerland, Southern Baptist Seminary in Louisville, Kentucky, and Baylor University in Waco, Texas). This experience, together with his work in Africa as both translations consultant and coordinator, gave him real empathy for the reader, and he was always open for suggestions as to how to make the text completely meaningful as well as faithful to the original.

Dr. John A. Thompson, known as "Jack" to his colleagues, was in age the "dean" of the committee but in appearance the most youthful. He had served for some twenty years as a missionary in Egypt (both his grandfather and father had been missionaries in Egypt) after brilliantly completing his studies in Old Testament under Professor William F. Albright at Johns Hopkins University. Jack, who had a working knowledge of some dozen ancient languages of the Near East, was a walking encyclopedia on the history and culture of biblical times.

In order to prepare a text of the *Good News Bible* for publication in Great Britain, the Reverend Brynmor F. Price of the British and Foreign Bible Society joined the work as "Her Majesty's Representative to the TEV Old Testament"—at least that was the way other committee members sometimes referred to "Bryn," as he is known to all his friends. He had had many years experience as a missionary in China and after that some years of work in India as a consultant on translational matters before joining the staff of the Translations Department of the British and Foreign Bible Society. His responsibility with the Old Testament Committee was to check on matters of British usage, including grammar, vocabulary, and spelling, and to arrange for certain editorial details in the British edition of the *Good News Bible*.

Mention of the committee's personnel would not be complete without including Mrs. Dorothy Ridgway of the Translations Department staff, who served as the committee's secretary. She looked after the coffee breaks, typed the entire manuscript of the Old Testament at least three times (in the case of some books even more than that), and sent out numerous copies to consultants and revisers. She also served as a "walking concordance" on orthographic details, it being her task constantly to check up on any inconsistencies in proper names, punctuation, and spelling.

At the beginning the committee held its sessions in New York City. This multiracial, multiethnic conglomerate—home of the United Nations, the Lincoln Center for the Performing Arts and the Metropolitan Art Museum, as well as the habitat of street gangs and burlesque shows—provided a backdrop for its work. "Common language" is certainly the principal form of English used by millions who live and work in this vast metropolis. Later, to be able to concentrate for longer periods of time in quieter surroundings, the translators met at various conference grounds, usually in off seasons. In such places they could effectively concentrate their efforts for as much as a month at a time and so work rapidly through some of the more complex aspects of their program. But the language of the metropolitan millions—bagel vendors, students, taxi drivers, shoeshine boys, secretaries, hotel clerks, waiters, executives, truck drivers, department store clerks, teachers, and subway trainmen—provided the framework for an ever-present awareness of those for whom this translation was being prepared.

In producing the basic draft of any book (called "stage 1" in the translation process), each translator was faced with three phases of work: (1) deciding upon the text of the Hebrew (or Aramaic for some chapters), (2) determining the meaning, and (3) expressing this meaning accurately on a common-language level. It would be impossible to list all of the many problems or even types of problems that one who translates from the Hebrew Old Testament encounters. The following two or three examples will give the reader some feeling for the complexity of the task.

Proverbs 11:30, which in the King James Version reads, "The fruit of the righteous is a tree of life; and he that winneth souls is wise," contains two problems in the Hebrew text itself. These are known as "textual problems." First, the term translated "righteous" is an abstract noun meaning "righteousness" in the Greek Septuagint version, a translation made from the Hebrew in ancient times. (The only difference in Hebrew between "righteous" and "righteousness" is the presence or absence of a very small letter called *yod*, comparable in size to an apostrophe.) Second, the Septuagint text has "violence" instead of "wise," reflecting the close resemblance of two Hebrew letters which were often mistaken for each other. There is a further problem with the meaning of the Hebrew expression here rendered "winneth souls," for nowhere else in the Bible does it have this meaning. In fact, elsewhere in the Old Testament this expression means "to take life," that is, "to kill," and this meaning fits precisely with "violence." Accordingly, the *Good News Bible* has followed the interpretation of most textual scholars and has translated this verse as "Righteousness gives life, but violence takes it away."

In the verse just considered, two problems of text combine with a problem of interpretation, but often the problem is one of how best to render a particularly difficult Hebrew expression, one which, if translated more or less word for word, could lead to serious misunderstanding on the part of the reader. For example, in the opening part of Amos 4:1 the Revised Standard Version reads "Hear this word, you cows of Bashan, who are in the mountain of Samaria." Reading this, a person might well suppose that the prophet Amos was somehow addressing cows who lived on a mountain. But from the context it is clear that Amos is talking to women who in some way or other are like cows. Furthermore, the reference to the fertile pastures of Bashan indicates that these women were growing fat through idleness and their constant indulgence in liquor supplied to them by their husbands (mentioned later in the same passage). The expression "mountain of Samaria" is only a way of referring to the city of Samaria; no real mountain was involved. Accordingly, in order to reflect more accurately the significance of the Hebrew passage, Today's English Version has "Listen to this, you women of Samaria, who grow fat like the well-fed cows of Bashan." Such a translation has a few more words than the original, but it contains no added meaning; it simply makes explicit what is clearly implicit in the immediate verbal context.

In addition to the three steps in the translation process, there were three stages through which the Old Testament text had to pass before the translation was complete and final. First, a draft translation had to be prepared on the basis of Kittel's *Biblia Hebraica*, the standard Hebrew text used in all scholarly activity. In preparing the draft translation of a particular Old Testament book, each member of the committee used data from a number of ancient versions (especially Greek and Latin), various commentaries, lexicons, and encyclopedias. In addition to making his translation, the translator prepared a series of notes to explain to other members of the committee just why he had adopted particular texts or renderings. This draft, together with the notes, was sent to Mrs. Ridgway, who made copies of them and sent the copies to the other members of the committee in order to obtain their written suggestions for improvements. When the translator received these suggestions from his colleagues, he collated them with his draft and carefully prepared for the next meeting of the full committee. At this meeting this particular draft would be up for discussion and the draft translator himself would be "sitting on the hot seat" (as the committee members themselves expressed it), since he would have to defend what he had done or help in the search for a better solution when his own solution to a specific problem was not acceptable to the other members of the committee.

In the committee sessions each translation was reviewed line by line, verse by verse, and even punctuation mark by punctuation mark. After the review was completed, the draft translator would read his revised translation aloud so that any expressions which might sound ambiguous or wrong to the ear, even though appearing all right to the eye, might be detected. For example, at one point in the process of translating the Psalms, a certain sentence read "Bring us back to our land, Lord." It looked all right on paper, but when it was read aloud, it was obvious that the comma after "land" would not suffice to keep the phrase from being heard as "Bring us back to our landlord."

When the committee had completed its review of this draft of the text, the results were then incorporated into a revised draft called "stage 2." Copies of this were sent out to various consultants and especially to translators working in various parts of the world. The text of stage 2, in fact, went to more than two hundred scholars and translators working in over sixty countries, and from many of these persons a

number of important suggestions came back. Then the translation went through essentially the same process that had been
used to refine the first draft. Now, however, the process was
much more rapid because nearly all the serious problems
had been resolved. The result of this second refinement was
"stage 3." Theoretically, the text was now ready for
publication.

In line with its regular procedure for the handling of major
texts of the Scriptures, the Bible Society sent the stage 3 text
to a special panel of eight biblical scholars, linguists, and
churchmen, representing seven different denominations. The
text was likewise submitted to an English stylistic review to
pick up matters of inconsistency in punctuation, awkward
shifts between series of relative pronouns, long strings of
unaccented syllables (especially in poetic sections), the incor-
rect placement of expressions of space and time, etc. Finally,
the Translations Committee of the American Bible Society
reviewed the text on behalf of the world fellowship of the
United Bible Societies.

Even when all this work had been completed, the text still
had to go to the Manuscript Department to be marked with
"specs" for the printers. That is, sizes and styles of type for
various sections had to be indicated; and also degrees of indentation (especially complex in the poetic passages), location of
footnote markers, and numerous other details had to be carefully specified and verified before composition could proceed
smoothly and accurately.

However, long before the entire Old Testament and a
revised fourth edition of the New Testament were ready for
the printers, a number of books of the Old Testament were
published, essentially as a means of testing the validity of the
translation and to stimulate the widest possible interest in the
work. The book of Psalms was published in December 1970;
by August 1971 the book of Job, with the title *Tried and
True,* was off the press. This was followed by Proverbs and
Ecclesiastes (*Wisdom for Modern Man*). The book of Jonah
(*The Man Who Said "No!"*) soon appeared, and Hosea, Amos,
and Micah were published together in booklet form under the
title *Justice Now!* Finally, Exodus appeared with the title
Let My People Go!

Some nine years after the work was begun, the text of the *Good News Bible* was off to the printers at last, but only because of the unusual gifts of a team of devoted men, who began each working day with the reading of Scripture and prayer and who constantly realized that it was only through the help of the Holy Spirit that they could hope to accomplish any lasting spiritual results. The Preface of the *Good News Bible* effectively captures that theme:

> No one knows better than the translators how difficult has been their task. But they have performed it gladly, conscious always of the presence of the Holy Spirit and of the tremendous debt which they owe to the dedication and scholarship of those who have preceded them. The Bible is not simply great literature to be admired and revered; it is Good News for all people everywhere—a message both to be understood and to be applied in daily life.

CHAPTER FIVE

New Meanings for Old

"If I only knew what it meant, I could translate it so much more easily," was how one missionary translator in Africa expressed his difficulties in dealing with one of the so-called "problem passages" in the Scriptures. "Problem passages" are those which can have more than one meaning and which have puzzled and perplexed biblical scholars throughout the centuries.

Among the most difficult of all such passages is Philippians 2:6b, which has been rendered traditionally as "Christ Jesus, who, being in the form of God, thought it not robbery to be equal with God." This traditional interpretation is seriously questioned by most biblical scholars. The principal difficulty centers on the Greek word *harpagmós*, which is found only in this verse. It occurs nowhere else in the Greek New Testament or in the Septuagint, the ancient Greek translation of the Old Testament. From earliest Christian times, commentators and expositors have argued about whether the word means (1) something to be kept by force or (2) something to be acquired by force. Clearly some concept of force is involved, but did Paul mean that Christ did not consider that equality with God was something to be acquired or something to be retained? The decision as to which interpretation to follow depends to some extent on determining the perspective which Paul may have had in mind. Was he, for example, thinking of Christ in his preincarnational state? In that case, the retaining of equality with God would fit well. Or was Paul picturing Christ in his incarnation? This is what seems to be implied in verses 7–9. In fact, it may well be that Paul is echoing a theme mentioned in Romans 5:15 and 1 Corinthians 15:21, in which Christ is contrasted with Adam, who indeed did try to become like God.

Accordingly, since the committee responsible for Today's English Version had adopted the principle of following in general the position of the majority of biblical scholars, they put in the text the rendering "he did not think that by force he should try to become equal with God." However, the alternative was put in the margin, "he did not think that by force he should try to remain equal with God." In either case, no doubt as to Christ's deity is implied, as the rendering of the following verse clearly indicates, "of his own free will he gave up all he had and took the nature of a servant." Paul's reasoning may well have been that since Christ was in fact equal with God, there was obviously no point in using force to become what he already was. With either interpretation the deity of Christ is unmistakably declared.

In the case of Romans 9:5, another "problem passage," scholarly opinion is perhaps even more divided, for in this instance the problem is one of punctuation. Unfortunately, there was no punctuation in ancient Greek manuscripts; in fact, there was not even any word division, so that the series of words which in Greek are literally, "Christ according to the flesh who being over all God blessed for ever," can be interpreted in several different ways. The two principal differences of interpretation are (1) the words "who being over all God blessed for ever" may be interpreted as referring to Christ, or (2) "who being over all . . . blessed for ever" may be considered as referring to God. In the first instance, the passage would be translated as "May he, who is God ruling over all, be praised forever," and in the second case, the rendering would be "May God, who rules over all, be praised forever." The Greek word order would appear to favor slightly the second interpretation, but, as in all such instances, the *Good News Bible* provides both renderings, one in the text and the other in the margin.

In many instances ambiguities which have existed in traditional translations are resolved in Today's English Version by a closer attention to the Greek text. In Ephesians 2:8 the King James Version has "For by grace are ye saved through faith; and that not of yourselves." Many persons have thought that the demonstrative pronoun "that" refers to "faith," so that not even "faith" was the result of man's own efforts. In reality, however, the Greek text indicates clearly that the reference here is not to "faith" alone but to the entire preceding clause, the fact of being saved by grace through faith. This is precisely what can only happen as the result of what God does through his Holy Spirit.

In other instances, what was formerly seen as an ambiguity of the Greek has been more carefully studied by scholars, and the result has been new spiritual insight and truth. In John 1:9 earlier translations have read, "That was the true light, which lights every man that comes into the world." This passage, however, speaks primarily of the entrance of the light, that is, the incarnation of Jesus Christ as the Word sent into the world. A more faithful and accurate translation is "This was the real light—the light that comes into the world and shines on all mankind."

Perhaps no rendering of Scripture has stirred more controversy and caused more consternation than the rendering in Isaiah 7:14 of "young woman" rather than "virgin." Almost instinctively some persons have thought that the change of "virgin" to "young woman" is an attack upon the doctrine of the virgin birth of Christ, while in reality the rendering of "young woman" actually enhances the uniqueness of the doctrine of Christ's virgin birth. If one were to insist upon "virgin" in Isaiah 7:14, it would be necessary to conclude that the Bible records two virgin births, which, of course, it does not. In Isaiah 7 the Lord tells King Ahaz to ask for a sign, and Ahaz refuses to put the Lord to the test; but the Lord insists on giving Ahaz a sign and assures him that by the time the child referred to is old enough to know the difference between good and evil, the two kings that Ahaz has dreaded will be deserted. This must have surely had meaning to King Ahaz, and it is interesting to note that the Hebrew term employed here, *almah,* is not the technical term for virgin (that would be *bethulah*), but designates any young woman of marriageable age and implies nothing as to a state of virginity. Moreover, in the Hebrew of this text the form of the verb "to conceive" is a participle, rather than a regular incompletive tense form, so that the more accurate translation is not "shall conceive" but "being with child" or "being pregnant." In keeping, therefore, with the evident meaning of this verse in the context of Isaiah 7, the *Good News Bible* has "a young woman who is pregnant will have a son and will name him 'Immanuel'." However, since the reasons for the difference between Isaiah 7:14 and Matthew 1:23 may not be understood, this marginal note is added: "The Hebrew word here translated 'young woman' is not the particular term for 'virgin,' but refers to any young woman of marriageable age. The use of 'virgin' in Matthew 1:23 reflects a Greek translation of the Old Testament, made some 500 years after Isaiah."

This note on Isaiah 7:14 is designed to explain to readers the fact that the New Testament reference in Matthew 1:23 is based upon the Septuagint Greek translation of the Old Testament, made some two hundred years before Christ. The seeming discrepancy between Matthew 1:23 and Isaiah 7:14 has bothered many readers of the Bible, but there is really no need for this. The Gospel of Matthew records the clear parallel which the early church readily recognized between the sign given to King Ahaz in Isaiah 7 and the virgin birth of Christ—a parallel made all the more obvious by the Septuagint rendering. This type of prophetic parallelism is often spoken of as "double fulfillment" or "double application" of prophecy. Another example is found in Matthew 2:15, where the clause "out of Egypt have I called my son" is employed as a reference to Christ, but in Hosea 11:1, from which these words are quoted, the reference is obviously to Israel.

By faithfully rendering the meaning of the Hebrew of Isaiah 7:14 and of the Greek of Matthew 1:23 ("a virgin will become pregnant and have a son"), the *Good News Bible* does justice to the meaning of the prophecy given to King Ahaz as well as to the announcement of the virgin birth of Christ, so unmistakably stated by Matthew. To have done differently would have been to make meaningless God's sign to Ahaz or to have required Christians to accept a doctrine of two virgin births. The virgin birth is further emphasized in the *Good News Bible* in Luke 1:34, which in traditional translations is rendered as "I do not know a man" (an expression open to various interpretations) but in Today's English Version as "I am a virgin."

Another passage of Scripture which has given rise to a number of different interpretations is Genesis 3:15, which in the King James Version is translated as "And I will put enmity between thee and the woman, and between thy seed and her seed; it shall bruise thy head, and thou shalt bruise his heel." This curse pronounced upon the serpent who tempted Eve has been variously interpreted, largely because of the collective expression "seed" and the pronominal reference "it." Following a Latin tradition, some exegetes have thought that the pronoun "it" should be changed to "she," thus referring to Mary. On the basis of the Hebrew text the conflict may be either between people and snakes or (more likely) between mankind and evil as symbolized by the serpent. Some persons would like to see in the pronoun "it" a direct reference to Christ, and accordingly they would interpret this verse as being a kind of proto-evangelium, that is, preview of the gospel.

If this passage is to be really meaningful to present-day English readers, it is clear that the term "seed" cannot be used. A possible equivalent would be "descendants," but the passage would then refer primarily to conflicts between people and snakes. In some way the collective sense of the Hebrew term does need to be preserved, and so the *Good News Bible* has "offspring." But "offspring" should not be understood merely in a singular sense, and so the entire verse is rendered as "I will make you and the woman hate each other; her offspring and yours will always be enemies. Her offspring will crush your head, and you will bite their heel."

Even the first verse of the Bible contains a very difficult problem of interpretation, for the Hebrew text can be rendered in several different ways. The traditional form, "In the beginning God created the heavens and the earth," is by no means the only way in which the Hebrew can be understood. It is also possible to interpret this first sentence as a dependent clause, "When God began to create the heavens and the earth," implying that in the beginning the earth was already "waste and void." In this verse there seems to be what some have regarded as a kind of "double focus" or "double emphasis." The first phrase can certainly be rendered as "in the beginning" (an expression echoed in John 1:1, "in the beginning was the Word"), but there is also a temporal element, and so in justice to these two elements in the text, Today's English Version has "In the beginning, when God created the universe."

Probably the most serious problem of interpretation for the first part of the Bible involves the Hebrew phrase *ruah elohim*, traditionally rendered as "Spirit of God" (Gen. 1:2). The difficulty with this phrase is that both *ruah* and *elohim* may have more than one meaning. *Ruah* may mean "breath," "wind," "spirit," and even "power" (especially in contexts where the "power" of God comes upon prophets). Likewise, *elohim* may have more than one meaning; it may mean "God," "gods," "mighty," and in some contexts even "angels" or "heavenly beings." Some biblical scholars, therefore, have felt that *ruah elohim* should be rendered as "mighty wind" (as, for example, in *The New English Bible*), on the assumption that all was chaos until God spoke his creative word. Other Bible exegetes prefer the traditional rendering "spirit of God" (or "Spirit of God"), but in the Old Testament the Hebrew phrase *ruah elohim* is rarely if ever associated with creation or physical phenomena; it is only in the New Testament that the full doctrine of the Holy Spirit becomes evident. Furthermore, in the New Testament Jesus Christ as "the Word," rather than the Spirit, is seen as the one through whom God creates. Accordingly, as an attempt to do justice to the extreme complexities of this passage, the *Good News Bible* reads "the power of God was moving over the water," and the various alternatives are listed in the margin.

Fortunately, most problems of interpretation are not so complex nor so sensitive theologically as those we have just cited. Nevertheless, there are other problem passages which in some ways may be even more relevant to Christian believers. "Be still, and know that I am God" (Ps. 46:10) has often been cited as an admonition to quiet meditation and the contemplative life, but in the context of this verse the psalmist has just been speaking of how God puts an end to war. The

Hebrew verb, which means "to cease an activity," ought to be translated in terms of this context; obviously the activity which must cease is war. In reality, therefore, God declares through the psalmist, "Stop fighting; and know that I am God." Is the Scripture trying to tell us that only when people stop their conflicts can they really come to know the presence and reality of God?

Some persons have argued that a translator should try to reproduce all ambiguities and obscurities in the biblical texts by being equally ambiguous and obscure in his renderings. Such a procedure would certainly be of no help to the reader. In many instances the reader would not recognize the existence of an ambiguity, and, even if he saw it, he would be likely to assume the wrong interpretation. Worse than that, a translator who proceeded in such a manner would do violence to the original text of Scripture. If one were to reproduce all the ambiguities and obscurities of the biblical texts, the impression would be given that the original writers did not really know what they were saying or that they were deliberately trying to be obscure and misleading. These writers, however, were not like the ancient Delphic oracles or modern fortunetellers who always try to protect their reputations by making double-tongued predictions. The biblical writers had important messages to proclaim, and they attempted to do so in clear, effective language. In most cases of ambiguity or obscurity, the trouble is not with the language of the biblical writers but rather with our ignorance of the situations in which they lived, the problems which they wrote about, and the ways in which people understood their declarations. If translators should attempt to straddle every exegetical fence with ambiguous renderings, they would seriously misrepresent the earnest intentions and driving concerns of the original writers. Present-day translators must simply acknowledge the existence of apparent differences of meaning by placing in the text those interpretations which seem to accord best with the findings of sound scholarship, and by providing the reader with the significant alternative renderings, so that he will be able to perceive at least something of the difficulties involved in understanding the original texts of Scripture.

CHAPTER SIX

New Words for Old Meanings

"But why change the Bible? We've come to love all those wonderful words" was the way one person protested the introduction of new words for old meanings in the *Good News Bible*. Such phrases as "gird up the loins of your mind," "tent of meeting," and even "only begotten" are not to be found in the *Good News Bible*, nor does one find such obsolete phrases as "We do you to wit" (2 Cor. 8:1) or "Thou shalt destroy them that speaking leasing" (Ps. 5:6).

The translators of the *Good News Bible* did not, however, introduce changes merely to be different or for the sake of novelty. If a traditional expression is accurate and readily understood by the average reader, it is retained, but where traditional words or phrases may not be clear or may even be misleading, then for the sake of faithfulness to the meaning of the original texts some changes have been introduced.

"Gird up the loins of your mind" (1 Pet. 1:13) is undoubtedly a striking Semitic idiom, but in present-day English it is almost totally meaningless. People no longer wear long, flowing garments which must be tightly fastened with a girdle before one can engage in rapid or energetic action. The meaning of this phrase is simply "have your minds ready for action," and that is precisely how Today's English Version renders it.

The phrase "tent of meeting," as a way of designating the ancient tabernacle, the center of worship for the Hebrews during their wandering in the wilderness, is for many readers a misleading expression. It suggests a meeting place, where the people normally gathered together or possibly where they

met to worship God. In reality, however, the Hebrew phrase
indicates that this was a place where the Lord met with his
people. This was where the Shekinah glory of the Lord's presence dwelt. Accordingly, the *Good News Bible* reads "the tent
of the Lord's presence."

When some readers do not find the term "only begotten" in
John 3:16, they assume that the translators imply a denial of
the doctrines of the deity and the virgin birth of Jesus Christ,
but such is by no means their intent. The traditional expression
"only begotten" arose from a misunderstanding of the original
Greek word *monogenēs*. This was carried over into the Latin
in the form of the word *unigenitus* (from *uni-* "one" and
-genitus "born"). But while the Greek *monō-* does mean
"only," *-genēs*, the second part of the word, does not derive
from *gennaō*, "to be born," but is related to *ginomai*, "to become." Thus *-genēs* means a "category" or a "kind," and
monogenēs really means "only one of its kind." That is precisely why this same term can be used in speaking of Isaac
(Heb. 11:17). Isaac was certainly not the only begotten son of
Abraham, for Abraham already had a son Ishmael before
Isaac was born, and later he had several sons by his wife
Keturah. But Isaac, as "the son of the promise," was the only
son of his kind, that is to say, a unique son. Similarly, Jesus
Christ is declared in John 3:16 to be the unique son of God,
his Son in a way that no one else is or can be. In using "only"
in place of "only begotten" Today's English Version not only
avoids the use of an obsolete term "begotten," no longer
understood by many people, but it emphasizes more effectively
the true nature of Christ's relation to God.

Some phrases are so familiar to regular Bible readers that
they seldom realize how strange these phrases must seem to
people who have not experienced a lifelong exposure to biblical
language. In Genesis 1:1 in place of "heavens and earth" the
Good News Bible reads "universe," a phrase which some
people think sounds too modern. But in present-day English
"heavens" occurs most often in such exclamatory phrases as
"heavens, yes!" or "good heavens!"; it has little to do with the
ancient concept of the sky. And to the modern speaker of

English the singular form "heaven" conveys a meaning very different from that of the plural "heavens."

Even more of a problem to many readers is the term "firmament," which has been used in many translations to refer to the celestial dome on which the stars and planets were supposedly fixed and on which the sun and moon moved in their orbits. This dome also contained the "windows of heaven" through which rain poured down upon the earth, but most importantly it served to separate the water which was above the dome from the water which was on the earth. For most persons today, however, "firmament" has little or no meaning. Some have even thought that it refers to the earth—something that is truly "firm."

For some persons one of the most surprising modifications in the *Good News Bible* is the change from "sinners" to "outcasts" in such passages as Mark 2:15, 17 and Luke 7:34. Surely, they argue, the Greek term *hamartōloi* should be translated as "sinners" in this passage, since that is what it normally means. But in passages speaking of "tax collectors and sinners," the reference is not simply to "bad people," but to those who had abandoned their identification with the Jewish religion and hence had been "cast out" or excommunicated from Jewish society.

In order to make the text of the Scriptures more meaningful and accurate, the *Good News Bible* contains a number of other departures from the wording which some people have long associated with the Bible. When the text speaks of God's vindication of his people, the word "vengeance" is used instead of "revenge." "Conscience" sometimes replaces "reins," which really means "kidneys." A literal translation of the Hebrew of Psalm 16:7 would in this context be entirely misleading. One would have to say "in the night my kidneys warn me." The term "leprosy" has a particularly unfortunate connotation in modern language. The term used in the Bible included a number of skin diseases in addition to what is technically known today as "leprosy." Therefore "dreaded skin disease" is a more accurate and meaningful rendering of the Hebrew term. Some readers of traditional versions have confused Noah's "ark" with "the ark of the covenant." Noah's ark was, of course, a comparatively large boat, and the ark of the covenant was a comparatively small box. Accordingly, that is what Today's English Version calls them, namely, "boat" and "box." Likewise, the "ark of bulrushes" in which the baby Moses was placed (Exod. 2:3) is called "a basket made of reeds." Furthermore, the term "ark," being almost unknown in the meaning of a boxlike object, is too readily understood by present-day readers as "arc."

Idioms have often been described as "the lifeblood" of a language, and translators are understandably reluctant to lose such effective vehicles of meaning. But when the original meaning of an idiom has been lost, with the result that people consistently misunderstand the figurative language of the original texts, it then becomes obvious, in the interests of accuracy and faithfulness to the meaning of the Scriptures, that such idioms must be sacrificed. In Amos there is a frequently repeated expression "for three transgressions . . . and for four" (Amos 1:3, 6, 9, 11, 13; 2:1, 4, 6), because of which the Lord declares that he will punish the various nations surrounding Israel. Many readers of the Bible have regarded the Lord's actions as entirely inexcusable. If these nations have erred only three or four times, why should they be punished so severely? In present-day English "three or four times" implies something which is relatively infrequent, for example, "he only did it three or four times." But in ancient Hebrew "for three . . . and for four" meant "over and over again," with the emphasis upon customary and habitual actions. Hence, in these passages in Amos the *Good News Bible* reads: "the people . . . have sinned again and again."

In many instances it is possible to retain a Hebrew or Greek idiom in translation, provided something of its significance is made explicit in the context. In Psalm 60:8 the clause "upon Edom I cast my shoe" might be interpreted by the average reader to mean that God simply despises Edom and is content to use it for nothing more than a box in which to toss dirty shoes or sandals. But in ancient times the casting of a shoe on something was a symbol of ownership, a custom which is reflected in Ruth 4:7, where the handing over of a sandal symbolized the transfer of legal ownership and rights. If the idiom in Psalm 60:8 is to be fully meaningful, it is necessary to supply the implicit information inherent in the context, "I will throw my sandals on Edom, as a sign that I own it."

Some idiomatic expressions may be well known, but may have lost their original meaning. This is precisely what has happened to the saying "Do not let your left hand know what your right hand is doing." In the Bible this is a warning against ostentation and show in providing for needy persons, but the saying has now come to mean something very different for many people. They interpret it to mean that, in doing something underhanded or illegal, it is important to keep no records. In this way one can even have a "lapse of memory" in court. In order to make certain that the real significance of Jesus' message is clear to the reader, the *Good News Bible* has employed the rendering "But when you help a needy person, do it in such a way that even your closest friend will not know about it." In present-day English this would be the equivalent of avoiding all "playing to the grandstands."

Changes in figurative expressions are obviously necessary when they no longer convey their original meanings, but alterations in the descriptions of actual historical events must not be introduced, even though the original significance of the act may have been lost. For example, there are frequent references in the Scriptures to someone's tearing his clothes, either as a sign of grief or of religious outrage. As in Matthew 26:65, the context helps to communicate the significance of the act, even though it may seem more psychotic than religious to present-day readers, for whom an idiom such as "blew his top" might be more typical.

Many translators of the Scriptures give in to the temptation to "modernize" the events of the Scriptures by substituting present-day parallels. For example, in the case of the Israelite cortege sent by King David to the Ammonites on the occasion of the death of King Hanun, one might want to speak of them as "tarred and feathered" rather than having half their beards shaved off and their skirts cut off at the hips, but being made

somewhat beardless as well as "pantless" seems disgrace enough
to present-day readers, even though it does not suggest all the
humiliation that David's emissaries must have felt.

There are, of course, contexts in which one can quite
appropriately employ modern equivalents which do full justice
to the original texts. In Acts 8:20 Peter's statement "Your
silver perish with you" made to Simon the magician, who
thought he could buy the power to convey the Holy Spirit to
others, sounds pathetically weak. The Greek text employs a
strong verb (*apollumi*) in such denunciations, and Peter's statement is far more faithfully and accurately rendered as "May
you and your money go to hell!"

Some persons have interpreted the principle of "dynamic
equivalence" as meaning any up-to-date expression which
carries impact and corresponds at least to some extent with the
original text, but such an interpretation of the principle is a
badly mistaken one. As mentioned earlier, the whole point of
dynamic equivalence is to make it possible for the present-day
reader to comprehend what the original reader must have
understood. The content of such a translation must hug the
ground of historical realism and fact—the circumstances of
time, place, and custom must be thoroughly and accurately
biblical—but in its form of language it must read insofar as
possible as though originally written in English, rather than in
Greek or Hebrew.

The extent to which this principle of dynamic equivalence
can and should influence translation may be illustrated by the
well-known Psalm 23 as it appears in the *Good News Bible:*

    1 The LORD is my shepherd;
          I have everything I need.
    2 He lets me rest in fields of green grass
          and leads me to quiet pools of fresh water.
    3 He gives me new strength.
      He guides me in the right paths,
          as he has promised.
    4 Even if I go through the deepest darkness,
          I will not be afraid, LORD,
          for you are with me.
       Your shepherd's rod and staff protect me.

  5 You prepare a banquet for me,
        where all my enemies can see me;
     you welcome me as an honored guest
        and fill my cup to the brim.
/ 6 I know that your goodness and love will be
        with me all my life;
     and your house will be my home as long
        as I live.

For those who have memorized this psalm in childhood, the
changes in wording may seem startling, if not somewhat
irreverent. But note briefly some of the problems of rendering
the meaning of the original text into present-day English.
Compare, for example, some of the traditional renderings:

(1) "I shall not want" can be understood as "the shepherd
whom I shall not want"; furthermore, "to want" now means "to
desire," not "to be in need." One could render the second line
as "I shall have need of nothing," but the positive statement is
not only clearer but more in keeping with the emphasis of the
original.

(2) "He makes me lie down" could be taken to mean "he
forces me to lie down," but the Hebrew form translated
"makes" really means "to permit," "to make possible," or "to
allow."

(3) "He restoreth my soul" sounds as though one's soul had
been lost and was later found. But the Hebrew term so often
translated as "soul" (*nephesh*) refers to the entire person, and
so "to restore the person" is to "give one new strength."

(4) "For his name's sake" is a particularly difficult idiom in
Hebrew. When rendered literally into English, it either has
very little meaning or suggests a wrong meaning, namely, that
the Lord does these things merely for his own selfish glory or
reputation. Since in Hebrew the term "his name" is so frequently used as a symbol for the Lord himself, as savior, pro-
tector, and creator, who has bound himself to his people by a
covenant, it seems more in keeping with the true sense of the
phrase to speak of the Lord's actions as reflecting his promises.

(5) "The valley of the shadow of death" has long been associated with the experience of death, but the Hebrew word

rendered "shadow of death" generally refers to intense darkness, and so it may be more appropriately and accurately rendered as "deepest darkness."

(6) "Comfort me" seems rather out of keeping in the context of "rod and staff," used by shepherds not to comfort sheep but to protect and defend them.

(7) "Anoint my head with oil" seems entirely strange to the present-day reader, for "oil" would only be understood as some kind of lubricant for engines and motors. Even "pouring olive oil on the head" would seem inappropriate—scarcely the way to honor a guest at a banquet. Therefore Today's English Version has shifted the figurative language to read "you welcome me as an honored guest," something which on one occasion a man who invited Jesus to his house failed to do (Luke 7:46).

One of the most extensive as well as subtle changes in Today's English Version reflects the concerns of the women's liberation movement. Some women are becoming increasingly disturbed by the frequent use of "man" or "men" in traditional translations when in reality the reference is to persons of both sexes. For example, in the book of Proverbs in the King James Version the word "man" or "men" occurs some 119 times, but only 5 of these are specific references to an adult male. In many instances it has been possible for the translators of the *Good News Bible* to use "persons," "people," "someone," "anyone," or "mankind" rather than "man" or "men," but in a number of contexts, especially those involving the relation, as well as the contrast, between God and "man," there is simply no way of avoiding the use of this term. One particularly useful means of avoiding the problem when the reference is to people in general is the shift from singular to plural. In Today's English Version the first part of Psalm 1, for example, reads "Happy are those who . . ." rather than "Happy is the man who. . . ."

These concerns of "women's lib" may in fact be in the direction in which some persons believe the English language is moving, but obviously the translators could never have accepted some of the extreme suggestions made by certain militants, who even wanted the pronoun "it" to be used in place of "he" when referring to God. Others have recommended "they" in referring to God, as a constant reference to the Trinity. Some have objected to the term "mankind" since it contains the component "man-"; and a few even reject the term "human," since they see the masculine "-man" hidden in this form.

The changes which the translators have introduced are not, however, attempts to placate an extreme minority; rather they reflect an effort to make the text as universally applicable as possible. When the linguistic forms are singular and particular, but the meaning is actually plural and general, then some modification is not only justified but even desirable.

CHAPTER SEVEN

Great Truths Made Clearer

A group of Sunday school teachers were asked to explain the meaning of the phrase "the righteousness of God" in Romans 1:17a, "the righteousness of God is revealed from faith to faith." They unanimously agreed that it must be God's own righteousness and goodness, but they admitted that this did not seem to fit in the verse which preceded nor even what followed. "But what else could it mean?" they asked. The phrase "from faith to faith" was even more obscure, for, as they said, "Whose faith is it? Are there two kinds of faith? Is it from God's faith to our faith?" And no one came up with a satisfying answer.

For this verse there is, however, general scholarly agreement that "righteousness" is not an abstract quality possessed by God, but refers to something which God himself does. Some believe that the reference is to "righting wrong," but most Bible scholars insist that this is what God does in putting people right with himself. This is the same Greek term which is sometimes translated "justification." Though an important biblical doctrine is involved, few people really understand it, since the word "justification" in present-day English rarely if ever corresponds to or even faintly reflects the meaning of the Greek term *dikaiosunē*. This term and the corresponding verb "to justify" do occur in modern English but not with anything like the biblical meaning. One may say "Joe was justified in what he did," meaning that though Joe's actions may have appeared to be wrong, he did in fact do what was right. "Justify" may also be used in speaking of "justifying accounts" or "justifying lines" (a term used in printing), but none of these meanings fits the biblical teaching.

The phrase "from faith to faith" in Romans 1:17 is even more obscure, for there seems to be no hint in the context as to whose faith is involved or how it is related to "righteousness." If, however, one takes "righteousness" as referring to God's putting people right with himself and "from faith to faith" as an idiomatic way of describing the fact that faith is involved from beginning to end, then one can justifiably translate the first part of this verse as "For the gospel reveals how God puts people right with himself; it is through faith from beginning to end." Now this vital statement becomes perfectly clear, and the meaning fits very well the preceding context, which speaks of Paul's complete confidence in the gospel (v. 16), as well as with the following quotation (v. 17b), which should be rendered as "The person who is put right with God through faith shall live." In this way principles of sound exegesis and dynamic equivalence combine to produce a translation of this crucial verse so that anyone and everyone may clearly understand.

When *Good News for Modern Man* was published, some readers said they were shocked not to find the word "propitiation" in 1 John 2:2. Was it possible that the translator did not believe in the "propitiation for sins"? What these persons did not sense was their own misunderstanding of the meaning of "propitiation," which really refers to the process of "making someone favorably inclined toward another." The English term "propitiation" might be described as a highbrow way of talking about arm-twisting, but there is no need for arm-twisting to get God on man's side. It was God who was in Christ reconciling the world to himself; Christ did not have to reconcile God to the world. The Greek noun *hilasmos* and the related verb *hilaskomai* never occur in the New Testament with God as the object, and in 1 John 2:2 it is not the propitiation of sin but the expiation of sin which is spoken of. For many readers, however, the term "expiation" would be even more difficult than "propitiation." In fact, both "expiation" and "propitiation," like "justification," "sanctification," and "predestination," are not much more than anglicized Latin. The words exist in dictionaries, but they are only very rarely heard in speech. Hence, if even the phrase "expiation of sins" is to be understood, it is much better rendered in 1 John 2:2 as "And Christ himself is the means by which our sins are forgiven." With this wording the vital message of this important verse becomes crystal clear.

Even more disturbed was a man who issued a 'statement asserting that "redemption has been completely removed from Today's English Version." It is true that the noun "redemption" is not used, but the verb "redeem" does occur, as in Revelation 14:4, and the noun "redeemer" occurs in Psalm 19:14. Moreover, the real meaning of the biblical concept of "redeem" and "redeemer" is expressed by other terms which represent even more faithfully the message of the Scriptures. The fact of the matter is that the terms "redeem" and "redemption" have lost very much of their earlier significance in English. For many people "redeem" is associated more with trading stamps than with the biblical theme of deliverance and salvation. In those contexts in which there is specific reference to the ancient practice of redeeming a slave through a payment, the *Good News Bible* makes this clear by rendering "God bought you for a price" (1 Cor. 6:20 and 7:23). But where the reference is to the way in which God delivers his people—as reflecting the experience of Israel in being rescued from Egypt—such words as "deliver," "save," or "rescue" are employed, for these terms express more clearly what God does in "setting free" his people.

There was a time in church history when theologians tried to insist that wherever the Greek term *apolutrōsis* occurs, it must be interpreted literally as "redemption," in the sense of making a payment. But then these theologians encountered major difficulties. To whom could God make such a payment? Driven by their own logic, these theologians could only conclude that God had to pay the devil in order to buy back people from his control. In pushing such an argument to its logical (or better, its illogical) extreme, they only succeeded in distorting the truth of God's intervention into history to deliver and save his people.

The term "saints" is another word which has lost much of

its real significance as the result of popular usage and miscon-
ceptions as to its true biblical meaning. For many people,
"saints" are only the patron saints of persons or institutions,
and as heavenly beings they are supposed to intercede for their
devotees. For others, "saints" are only those specially devout
and holy persons who are often more sanctimonious than
sanctified. In his first letter to the Corinthians, Paul addresses
the "sanctified" and indicates that they were called to be
"saints," while in his second letter the apostle addresses them
as "saints," but obviously he wants them to be far more consecrated to the work and worship of God than they as yet are.
In order to reproduce more faithfully the meaning of the Greek
term traditionally translated "saints," it is much better to speak
of "the people of God," even as Today's English Version does.
They have not always been fully consecrated or sanctified, but
they do belong to God, and as his people they are the objects
of his constant concern and love.

No doubt the most controversial issue concerning *Good
News for Modern Man* has been what some persons have
alleged to be "the total omission of the blood." It is, of course,
simply not true that references to the blood of Christ have
been omitted. Wherever there is a clear reference to Christ's
blood, either in the shedding of it or as represented by the symbolic blood of the Old Testament sacrifices, the term "blood"
does occur in Today's English Version. See, for example, John
6:53–56. In Hebrews 9:14 ("his blood will purify our con-
sciences"), 10:29 ("who treats as a cheap thing the blood of
God's covenant"), 13:12 ("in order to purify the people from
sin with his own blood"), 1 John 1:7 ("the blood of Jesus, his
Son, purifies us from every sin"), as well as in a number of
other similar types of passages, the Greek term *haima* is rendered as "blood," for in all these contexts there is a clear reference to blood as a symbolic element in the sacrifice of Jesus. In
all references to the Lord's Supper (Matt. 26:28; Mark 14:24;
Luke 22:20; 1 Cor. 10:16; 11:25, 27) the term "blood" also
occurs since the blood of Christ is the symbol of his sacrificial,
redemptive death for men.

It would be a serious mistake, however, to assume that
wherever the Greek term *haima* occurs, it should always be

translated "blood," since in many instances it has quite a different meaning. In Matthew 27:24–25 Pilate washes his hands and says to the crowd, "I am innocent of the *haima* of this man." Quite clearly Pilate is referring to Jesus' forthcoming execution, and when the crowd shouts back, "May his *haima* be upon us and our children," the reference is to their demand for Jesus' death. For this reason the *Good News Bible* renders Pilate's statement as "I am not responsible for the death of this man" and the crowd's response as "Let the punishment for his death fall on us and on our children." In other instances *haima* may be more accurately rendered as "murder." Matthew 23:35 ("That upon you may come all the righteous blood shed upon the earth, from the blood of righteous Abel unto the blood of Zacharias son of Barachias, whom ye slew between the temple and the altar") is more meaningfully and accurately translated as in Today's English Version: "As a result, the punishment for the murder of all innocent men will fall on you, from the murder of innocent Abel to the murder of Zechariah son of Berechiah, whom you murdered between the Temple and the altar." Instead of "righteous blood," a very complex figurative expression, it is much more accurate to speak about "innocent men."

The term "blood" may even be used to speak of spiritual, rather than physical, death. In Acts 18:6 Paul declares to the Jews in Corinth that their "blood" is on their own heads, but he is obviously not speaking about their physical death. Accordingly, the *Good News Bible* has "If you are lost, you yourselves must take the blame for it!" Likewise, in Acts 20:26 Paul warns the Ephesian elders that he was literally "innocent of the blood of all," but the meaning is quite clear: "If any of you should be lost, I am not responsible."

A further complication in the translation of Greek *haima* is that the associated phrase "shed blood" normally refers to "shedding someone else's blood" rather than "shedding one's own."

Since Greek *haima* clearly does not always mean literally "blood" but refers often to death as such, the real question is how to translate the term in those eleven passages which speak of the redemptive death of Christ (Acts 20:28; Rom. 3:25; 5:9; Eph. 1:7; 2:13; Col. 1:20; Heb. 10:19; 13:20; 1 Pet. 1:19; and

Rev. 1:5; 5:9). To translate *haima* as "blood" in Acts 20:28
(as in traditional translations, "to feed the church of God
which he purchased with his own blood") could give the impression that Christ's blood became an object of barter, as
though focus were on the substance of the blood rather than
on the death of the person, for which the substance is a figurative substitute. The figurative character of this verse is made
even more evident by the figurative use of the word "purchased," for clearly God did not buy his church from anyone;
the church became his possession through the atoning death
of Christ. Accordingly, the *Good News Bible* reads: "Be shepherds of the church of God, which he made his own through
the death of his Son."

By rendering *haima* as "death," Colossians 1:20 also becomes much clearer. In traditional translations the reference is
to God as "having made peace through the blood of his cross."
The Greek text is so succinct as to be somewhat confusing. In
reality, there are two figurative expressions in Colossians 1:20
even as there are in Acts 20:28. In this verse in Colossians,
"blood" stands for "death" and the "cross" stands for "cruci-
fixion." To make the meaning clear and to reflect faithfully
the sense of the Greek text, the *Good News Bible* has "God
made peace through his Son's death on the cross." Rather
than robbing the Scriptures of meaning, as some persons have
supposed, to render *haima* as "death" in certain passages actually emphasizes the significance of Christ's atoning death.

Perhaps one of the most misunderstood elements in traditional translations is the use of "fear" in such phrases as "fear
the Lord" and "fear God." In present-day English the term
"fear" in such contexts could only mean "to be afraid of" or
"to be scared of," but obviously this is not the sense in most
passages of the Bible, and so Sunday school teachers constantly have to tell their children that when the Bible speaks
of "fearing the Lord" it really means to have reverence for
him. For example, the traditional translation of Psalm 147:11,
"The Lord taketh pleasure in them that fear him, in those that
hope in his mercy" (KJV), is very misleading. The Lord is
surely not a bogeyman who is pleased when people are scared
of him.

The Hebrew expressions which have been customarily translated as "fear" are often better rendered in a number of different ways, depending upon the context. For example, in Exodus 20:20 an accurate equivalent is "obey," though in Nehemiah 5:15 "honor" expressed the thought better and in Psalm 118:4 "worship" is more appropriate. In Job 25:2 and 37:24 the Hebrew expressions can be rendered as "to stand in awe of," while in Psalm 147:11 the *Good News Bible* speaks of the Lord as "taking pleasure in those who honor him."

Such substitutes of more accurate renderings for "fear" do not mean that the verb "fear" has been eliminated from the Scriptures. In certain contexts it is entirely appropriate and so it remains. But the use of more accurate renderings of the Greek and Hebrew terms is a big step forward in making the Bible more meaningful to people and more faithful to its vital message.

In the view of some persons, to render the same Greek or Hebrew terms by several different expressions in English is a dangerous thing to do. For one thing, it appears to reflect inconsistency on the part of the translators and the introduction of subjective judgments. The translators of the King James Version faced this same problem, and they felt it was necessary to anticipate this type of objection, for they themselves refused to produce a strictly literal, "concordant" translation in which each Greek or Hebrew word was consistently rendered by a single corresponding English term. They expressed their principle of translation both exquisitely and sharply in their "Preface to the Reader":

> Another thing we think good to admonish thee of (gentle Reader) that we have not tyed our selves to an uniformitie of phrasing, or to an identitie of words, as some peradventure would wish that we had done. . . . Thus to mince the matter, we thought to favor more of curiosity (pedantry) than wisedom . . . .For is the Kingdome of God become words or syllables? Why should we be in bondage to them if we may be free, use one precisely when we must use another no less fit. . .?

Though some persons think that the failure to translate a particular Greek or Hebrew term by a single English word betrays a lack of consistency, the truth is that only by using different words to express the different meanings of the original terms can one really be consistent with the sense of the various passages. If we were translating from English into another language, we would never expect a translator to always render the English word "bar" by a single corresponding term. No language could possibly have a single term to express all the different meanings attached to this word, among which are "a bar of soap," "a candy bar," "he was admitted to the bar," "he put a bar across the window," "she was standing by the stocking bar," "he has a bar in his living room," "he hangs out in the bar," and "his past deeds were no bar to his getting the job." If in translating from English into Spanish one has to use at least six different words to represent the diverse meanings of English "bar"—and that is precisely the case—it is no wonder that one must similarly render some Greek and Hebrew terms by a corresponding series of different expressions in English.

CHAPTER EIGHT

Making Sense Out of Nonsense

"What under the sun is a pygarg?" exclaimed one man as he read Deuteronomy 14:5; but that was only the beginning of trouble, for on the next page of his Bible, he ran into the terms "ossifrage" and "glede." What is a translator to do when he runs into terms in the original language whose meanings have been forgotten or are in considerable doubt? Should he conform to tradition and produce something that practically no one can understand? Or should he try to make sense out of what for so many people is just "non-sense"? Trying to make sense in such cases is certainly not easy; in fact, it is just here that the translator's scholarship, ingenuity, and resourcefulness are stretched to the limit. In the case of many ancient Hebrew terms, no one today really knows just what their meanings are. That is especially true of those which may occur only once in the entire Old Testament and for which no cognates have been discovered in related languages such as Syriac and Arabic.

In the case of Deuteronomy 14:5, probably the most sensible way of speaking about certain so-called "clean animals" is to list them as "deer, wild sheep, wild goats, or antelopes." Likewise in verses 12–18 of the same chapter one can only list various major kinds of birds, such as "eagles, owls, hawks, falcons, buzzards, vultures, crows, ostriches, seagulls," etc. To be more specific than that would result in lists of terms entirely unknown to the average reader or in speculative identifications which might be quite misleading.

The words "cubit" and "shekel" are no doubt better known

to the average speaker of English than "pygarg," "ossifrage," and "glede"; but how much meaning do these convey to the mind in terms of linear measure and monetary values? A cubit is approximately a foot and a half or 18 inches (traditionally, from the fingertips to the elbow), so it is quite possible to calculate in feet a biblical measurement given in cubits, but when it comes to "shekels" the problems are more complex. At first the "shekel" was a unit of weight, but later the term was used to designate money also (like the term "pound" in English). In early Babylonian times the shekel weight varied from 8 to 16 grams, or about 0.3 to 0.6 ounces. But in Israelite times the shekel averaged about 11 grams or approximately 0.4 ounces. But these are only averages, and there were rather extensive variations. In speaking of Goliath's armor (1 Sam. 17:5) it makes little sense to talk about "5,000 shekels" or "2,000 ounces," for one never speaks of armor in terms of ounces. The translators, therefore, used the approximate equivalent in pounds. Saying that the armor weighed "125 pounds" and that the iron head of Goliath's spear weighed "15 pounds" immediately conveys some idea of their weight to the modern English reader.

The concept of a "talent" as an amount of money is extremely vague, while "talent" as a measure of weight is practically meaningless to the ordinary reader of English. For most of these people the term is used only in reference to some special skill or aptitude. In Mesopotamia and Canaan of biblical times the term was used as a large measure of weight. The amount varied through the centuries, but it may be considered as equivalent to about 75 pounds in New Testament times. A talent of silver was worth some 6,000 denarii, equivalent to what a common laborer might earn in twenty-four years. In the parable of the talents Jesus was speaking about very large sums of money. No wonder the master of the lazy servant was angry when he learned that his money had not been deposited with the money-lenders so that it would at least earn interest. With the present-day fluctuations in so many currencies one can scarcely speak in terms of francs, marks, pesos, yen, cruzeiros, baht, rupees, or dollars. In some instances the figures given would lose their true significance in the space of a year or two, perhaps less. Therefore, in the parable beginning at Matthew 25:14, instead of the traditional ten talents, five talents, and one talent, the *Good News Bible* has "five thousand silver coins . . . two thousand . . . one thousand."

In many instances it is not possible to state in the text the exact amount of money involved, and it is really not necessary to do so, for it is the contrast in values, rather than specific amounts, which is important. The ten thousand talents in Matthew 18:24 would certainly be a huge sum in terms of dollars, but what is important is the difference between the ten thousand talents and the hundred denarii of verse 28. Accordingly, the *Good. News Bible* has "millions of dollars" in contrast with "a few dollars." Some persons have scoffed at this parable; they have reasoned that no servant, certainly no slave, would ever be entrusted with millions of dollars. In ancient times, however, some persons who had been taken captive in war were kept as managers of their large business enterprises. In slave auctions such a slave, together with his business, might be sold for the equivalent of millions of dollars. In fact, some slaves of the Romans had such a high price set on them that only partnerships (the equivalent of present-day corporations) were able to buy them.

In many ways the measurement of time in the Bible is as complicated as the measures of money, and equally misleading if translated literally. In the ancient world the day was divided into twelve hours, and these were numbered from sunrise, so that the "third hour" would be around nine o'clock in the morning, and "the sixth to the ninth hour" would be from twelve noon until three in the afternoon. Unless one makes adjustments in expressions of time, the biblical accounts often sound quite strange. There are even some instances in which there seems to be no way to resolve apparent discrepancies. For example, in John 19:14 the "sixth hour" must be consistently rendered as "noon." Some persons have thought that perhaps there were two systems for reckoning time in the ancient world, one used by the Romans and the other by the Jews, but there is no real evidence for such a distinction. To be faithful to the Greek text, one can only say "noon."

References to days of the week are sometimes even more

complicated, since for the Jews a new day began at sunset and ended with the sunset of the following day. In Acts 20:7–12 Luke describes Paul's meeting with the Christians in Troas and the long evening service "on the first day of the week, when the disciples came together to break bread." The first day of the week was then Sunday, as it is today (although many people are beginning to speak of Monday as the first day of the week and of Sunday as the end of the week). The "first day" mentioned by Luke was probably thought of as beginning at sunset, not at midnight as we would normally suppose today. Hence, the meeting at which Paul spoke so long that the young man Eutychus fell asleep and toppled out of a third-story window, evidently took place on what in present-day language would be "Saturday evening," the beginning of the first day of the new week. It is possible, of course, that Sunday was involved, and so this alternative is given in a footnote.

Some traditional biblical terms are known well enough, but only in meanings which are quite inappropriate for the contexts in which they formerly occurred. For example, "cherub" is now rarely recognized as the singular of "cherubim," those winged creatures which sheltered the ancient Covenant Box or who stood guard at the entrance to the Garden of Eden. A cherub has become a roly-poly, naked (or nearly naked), little angelic being, a first cousin of Cupid with his bow and arrow. In the meantime, "cherubim" has become for many persons a singular noun, for which the plural is "cherubims." In the *Good News Bible* the cherubim are more meaningfully referred to as "winged creatures" when the context involves a graphic representation and as "living creatures" when the context suggests a supernatural being. A note in the Word List calls attention to the various descriptions of these creatures in Exodus 25, Ezekiel 1, and Revelation 4.

Strange proper names also pose problems for both readers and translators, especially when the same object or person may be referred to by more than one name. In the New Testament the names "Prisca" and "Priscilla" refer to the same woman, and "Timothy" and "Timotheus" identify the same man, so the *Good News Bible* has consistently used only one form of the name when it refers to one and the same individual. This is not done, of course, when in the biblical narrative itself a specific change is made in the name of a person, as in the shift from the name "Abram" to "Abraham." A particularly confusing shift of names occurs in traditional translations of Acts 7:45 and Hebrews 4:8. The "Jesus" of these passages is a reference to Joshua in the Old Testament, the English name "Jesus" being based on the Greek transcription of the Hebrew name "Joshua." But the ordinary English reader is confused when he reads in Acts 7:44–45 that the tabernacle was brought into the Holy Land "with Jesus." Again, the ordinary reader would not know that the names "Jeconiah" (Jer. 24:1) and "Coniah" (Jer. 37:1) are variations on the name of the king of Judah usually called "Jehoiachin." This would not be a particularly serious misunderstanding because King Jehoiachin is a relatively minor figure in Jewish history. As indicated in the. Preface to the *Good News Bible*, its translators have chosen to use consistently that form of a particular name which is most widely used and known. In some instances the two (sometimes more) names of a person are so different as to make it impossible to determine which should be employed, especially when the different forms are not mere spelling variations. For example, in 2 Chronicles 34:20 "Abdon son of Micaiah" is mentioned, while in 2 Kings 22:12 this same person is called "Achbor." There is no way to determine which name should have precedence, and so both names are used in the text, and a footnote calls attention to the difference.

Problems of consistency in the forms of proper names also involve the names of geographical objects. Mount Sinai is sometimes referred to in Scriptures as "Mount Horeb," but it seems preferable to preserve the better known term in order to avoid unnecessary confusion for the reader. Similarly, the "Mediterranean Sea" is sometimes spoken of as the "Great Sea," but its more common designation is used throughout the *Good News Bible*. The same kind of difference occurs with "Salt Sea" and "Dead Sea." The latter is used in the *Good News Bible* because it is the more commonly used name today. A more difficult problem is involved in the speaking of the "Red

Sea." This body of water, including the Gulf of Aqaba, the Gulf of Suez, and the marshy lakes between the Gulf of Suez and the Mediterranean are all referred to in the Old Testament by a name which is literally translated "Sea of Reeds." This name no doubt originated as a designation of the marshlands between Egypt and Palestine and was later extended to include other areas. It would, however, be quite confusing to speak in the Old Testament of the people of Israel as "crossing the Sea of Reeds" but in the New Testament of their "crossing the Red Sea." The possible confusion in these Old Testament and New Testament expressions is briefly explained in the Word List.

Many geographical names in the Old Testament have meanings which can form the basis for somewhat more vivid designations. For example, "Abel-shittim" may be rendered as "Acacia Valley," the "Arabah" is better referred to as "Jordan Valley," and the "Valley of Achor" may be called "Trouble Valley." "Helkath-hazzurim" actually means "Field of Swords" and "Allon-bacuth" is literally "Oak of Weeping." When the meaning of a proper name is especially appropriate to the context, its meaning is generally represented in an English equivalent rather than being merely transliterated.

There are instances, on the other hand, in which certain geographical names have lost their geographical significance. For example, the phrase "ships of Tarshish" does not always indicate ships coming from or going to Tarshish, presumably an important ancient seaport in Spain; often it simply means "ocean-going ships." Likewise, "the gold of Ophir" does not always refer to gold that has come from Ophir, but rather to "pure gold," much in the same way that "cheddar cheese" no longer refers to cheese that has been made in the village of Cheddar in England, but to a particular kind of cheese.

Some proper names are much better translated on the basis of their referents, so that the terms "Rephaim" and "Nephilim" are "giants," and "Sheol" is "the world of the dead."

On the other hand, the Hebrew term *asherah* has often been translated as "sacred poles" or "pillars," but these were actually symbols of the fertility goddess Asherah. Hence it is more meaningful to render this term as "symbols (images) of the goddess Asherah." The Word List contains a further explanation about this fertility goddess.

Perhaps the greatest difficulty with traditional translations is that present-day readers are usually not aware of the changes in meaning which have occurred through the centuries. They may instinctively feel that "charity" in 1 Corinthians 13 is not really appropriate, but they do not know that when that English word was first used (a borrowing from the Latin *caritas*) it was an appropriate equivalent of Greek *agapē,* "love." During the centuries, however, "charity" has come to mean only giving help to the poor. Another example of such changes in meaning is the term "brazen." Originally it was used to designate anything made of brass, but it is now used almost exclusively to speak of a certain trait of personality, as in "he has a brazen attitude."

Some shifts of meaning actually involve a coalescing of what were originally two quite distinct words. In the King James Version, 2 Thessalonians 2:7 reads: "For the mystery of iniquity doth already work: only he who now letteth will let, until he be taken out of the way." Even some preachers have assumed that this means that the Holy Spirit has given permission for the mystery of iniquity to be active in the world, but that is not at all the case. The English word "let" meaning "to permit" originally had a distinctly different vowel from the word "let" meaning "to prevent." The meaning "let" in the sense of "to prevent" is still preserved in the legal expression "without let or hindrance." It also lingers in the tennis phrase "let ball." This originally meant a hindered ball, that is, one which had struck the net; but because "let" in this sense of hindrance is no longer known, many tennis players have changed the expression to "net ball."

Fortunately, not all shifts of meaning are as misleading as in the case of "let," but there are still some persons who think that "divers diseases" must refer to the "bends" ("diver's disease"!) and that "the last trump" is somehow related to a card game!

In trying to make sense of what must often seem to be nonsense, a translator must constantly beware of using anachronisms, that is, expressions which would be out of place in the course of time. In 2 Samuel 1:21 there is a reference to Saul's shield lying exposed on the hills of Gilboa. A translator might be tempted to use a present-day English expression and say "it lay rusting," but this would assume that Saul's shield was made of iron. In the time of Saul, however, shields were made of leather. It is possible that bronze was sometimes used, but shields were certainly not made of iron. Furthermore, the Hebrew text speaks of the shield as "no longer anointed with oil," a reference no doubt to the use of oil to keep the leather in condition. To speak of a "rusting shield" would certainly imply the use of iron implements of war in the earlier bronze culture.

In making sense out of nonsense, a translator must always make certain to make the right sense.

CHAPTER NINE

Older and Better Texts

Nothing is more disconcerting for the Bible reader than to find a well-known passage of Scripture missing from a new translation. A Zulu leader from South Africa on a special government tour of the United States requested that one of his first stops be at the Bible House in New York. He wanted to find out why the words "For thine is the kingdom and the power and the glory forever. Amen" are not found in his Zulu Bible. Roman Catholics have been accused of tampering with the Scriptures because this clause does not appear in Matthew 6:13 in their Bibles; and some Protestants have supposed that these words may have been omitted in some so-called "Protestant Bibles" as a concession to Roman Catholics. The fact is that this clause does not occur in Jerome's famous Latin translation known as the Vulgate, traditionally the standard Bible of the Roman Catholic Church. An even better reason for its omission in various translations is that it does not occur in the oldest and best Greek manuscripts.

There are some persons, however, who have argued that this ending to the Lord's Prayer should be included in translations simply because it occurs in such a large number of manuscripts. It is certainly true that if the correctness of texts must be determined merely on the basis of counting manuscripts, then that ending should be inserted. But what really matters is not so much the number of manuscripts as their integrity and their antiquity. The oldest manuscripts are much more likely to be closer to the original text, since they are much less likely to have suffered from either unintentional errors or intentional additions on the part of copyists. The fact that a great many manuscripts are found to have a particular form of text is not very meaningful if it is evident that they all were copied from the same source. And since we do not have any original autographs (that is, manuscripts which came directly from their original authors), scholars must judge the value of different manuscripts on the basis of the range of early evidence and not on the basis of mere numbers or tradition. The confidence of Christians in the Bible has always been based upon its divine authority and not upon the infallibility of the scribes who made handwritten copies of it.

The omission of the well-known ending to the Lord's Prayer is supported by the best of the early manuscripts, including the manuscript found by Count Tischendorf at Mount Sinai, the Vaticanus manuscript, and the Codex Bezae, a so-called Western Text, by the Old Latin and Coptic versions, and many of the early Church Fathers—an array of textual evidence rarely equaled.

In early Christian times many different persons must have felt the need for some more liturgical ending to the prayer, and several different forms did, in fact, develop, all of which suggests that originally there was no ending at all. Surely no scribe would have omitted such an ending if it had been there originally.

One passage with even far less textual evidence is 1 John 5:7b–8a, the passage about the "three heavenly witnesses," namely, "the Father, the Word, and the Holy Ghost." This passage is absent from every known Greek manuscript, except four, and these are from the eleventh century or later and appear to be translations of the Latin rather than copies of earlier Greek manuscripts. Furthermore, two of these manuscripts have the passage only in the margin. It is not quoted by any of the Greek Fathers and it is not found in the manuscripts of any of the ancient versions with the exception of the Latin. Even in the Latin manuscripts it does not appear until the latter part of the fourth century. Some persons have felt that the omission of this passage damages seriously the doctrine of the Trinity, but if belief in the Trinity were based only or even primarily on this passage, such an important doctrine of the Christian church would rest on a very weak foundation indeed. The doctrine of the Trinity was strongly and effectively defended by early church theologians, who evidently had no knowledge whatsoever of this passage. Obviously they were quite able to defend their position without it in the great Sabellian and Arian controversies.

Some of the textual problems involving additions are the result of what is called "harmonization." That is a tendency of scribes to make the text at one place in Scripture harmonize with the text in another place. Sometimes it was consciously done by a well-meaning copyist who, remembering the reading in another place, probably thought that the passage at hand was defective. At other times it may have been done unconsciously when the memory of the scribe was more alert than his eyes. An example of harmonization is found in the form of the Lord's Prayer in Luke. Since the form of the prayer in Matthew was apparently so much better known and more wisely used, it is not strange that some scribes tended to supply expressions from Matthew while making copies of Luke. Perhaps they thought that earlier scribes had for some reason or other omitted certain words or phrases. Accordingly, they wrote "Father in heaven" in place of simply "Father," and they added "Thy will be done, as in heaven, so on earth." Interestingly enough, these scribes did not add to Luke's form of the prayer the ending which became associated with the Matthean form.

In Colossians 1:14 some early scribe added the words "through his blood" after "in whom we have redemption" on the basis of the completely parallel expression found in Ephesians 1:7. The textual evidence for this addition in Colossians is so limited that the problem is not even mentioned in the Greek New Testament published by the United Bible Societies and edited by an international and interconfessional team of outstanding New Testament Greek scholars.

In a few instances some scribes apparently wished to avoid statements which might seem inappropriate or inconsistent with the contents of other passages of Scripture. In Luke 2:33 they changed "his father" to "Joseph," and in 2:43 they changed "his parents" to "Joseph and his mother." Interestingly enough, however, similar changes were not made in Luke 2:41, where the reading is "parents" in all manuscripts, and in 2:48 which quotes Mary as saying "your father and I." These renderings are not, of course, to be interpreted as reflecting in any way upon the doctrine of the virgin birth. Luke makes quite clear the miraculous nature of Jesus' birth in Luke 1:27, 34, 35, and 2:5.

In a few instances the earlier, better Greek texts have a somewhat longer reading than the later ones on which traditional translations have been based. In 1 Peter 2:2b the King James Version reads "that ye may grow thereby," but the *Good News Bible,* based on better Greek manuscript evidence, reads "that you may grow up and be saved."

When scribes had to copy manuscripts, they would sometimes inadvertently omit a line, especially if two succeeding lines began or ended with the same words. Such textual errors are easily detected and corrected, but much more complicated are those alterations which got into the text when scribes wrote from dictation. By New Testament times new manuscripts were sometimes mass-produced by having one person read a text aloud while several copyists wrote down what they heard. However, the pronunciation of several vowels and diphthongs of the Greek language which had been quite distinct in the classical period gradually changed, so that by the first century A.D. the distinctiveness had disappeared; their sounds had "fallen together." This was especially a problem with the pronouns for "we" and "you" (plural), which sounded the same. As a result, there are a large number of manuscript variations at places where the Greek words for "we" and "you" are involved, and sometimes it is impossible to determine which was the original word. For example, in 2 Corinthians 8:7 it is impossible to know whether one should read "your love for us" or "our love for you," and so the *Good News Bible* lists both possibilities, putting one in the text and the other in the margin.

It sometimes happens that lurking behind an apparently anomalous textual difference there may even be a distinction of words in still another language, for it is likely that the major part of Jesus' public ministry and some of the narratives concerning it were in the Aramaic language, so that what was recorded in Greek was already a translation from an earlier oral source. For example, in Mark 1:41 the textual evidence is almost evenly divided between two Greek verbs which have entirely different meanings. In the one case Jesus would be described as "having compassion" (or "pity") on the leper who pled to be healed, and in the other case Jesus would be said to "be indignant" (or "angry") with the leper. *The New English Bible* translates the Greek term with "indignation" but tones down this meaning by adding "warm." It is possible that the term meaning "anger" was suggested by a similar type of expression in verse 43, translated by NEB as "spoke sternly to him." But it is also possible that underlying these two quite different verbs in Greek are two Aramaic words which would be very similar in pronunciation (compare, for example, the Syriac *ethraham* "he had pity" with *ethra'em* "he was enraged").

Scholars dealing with the text of the Greek New Testament are often overwhelmed, if not embarrassed, by the abundance of evidence from ancient sources, including well over two hundred important manuscripts, both in Greek as well as in various ancient versions, and some five thousand additional manuscripts which must be evaluated to determine if they have relevant textual evidence. But, while the textual problems of the New Testament are complicated because of the abundance of evidence, the textual difficulties of the Old Testament become particularly acute because of the scarcity of evidence. There are, of course, certain minor differences even among the so-called Massoretic manuscripts, which received their standard form by the ninth century A.D. Also, within the Massoretic tradition there are a number of differences between what was retained in the written form of the text (called the "kethib") and what was recommended for actual oral reading (called the "qere"). As a supplement to the Massoretic tradition one can compare the Samaritan text for the Pentateuch, and there are also the ancient Targums (combinations of text and brief commentary). The Septuagint translation, made from Hebrew into the Greek language about two hundred years before Christ, often sheds some light on textual difficulties, and the literal Greek translations of Aquila, Theodotian, and Symmachus are sometimes helpful. Jerome's Latin translation, which was made directly from the Hebrew, is also valuable. More recently, discoveries of Hebrew manuscripts in the caves at Qumran near the Dead Sea have pushed back Hebrew textual evidence almost a thousand years, and their principal value has been to confirm the remarkable accuracy and integrity of the Massoretic textual tradition.

To deal with some of the particularly difficult textual problems of the Old Testament, the United Bible Societies have brought together an international team of specialists who are highly competent in matters pertaining to ancient Hebrew. These scholars have been doing for the text of the Old Testament what a similar group of scholars did some time ago for the text of the New Testament. They are compiling a series of highly important recommendations for translators as to what could and should be done in treating some of the textually difficult passages of the Hebrew Scriptures.

One of the confusing passages in the Old Testament is Genesis 4:8, which reads in the King James Version: "And Cain talked with Abel his brother: and it came to pass, when they were in the field, that Cain rose up against Abel his brother, and slew him." There seems to be a real gap in the sequence of events. First, Cain is simply speaking with Abel, and then in the field he attacks his brother. But in the Septuagint, Syriac, and Vulgate versions (as well as in some Hebrew manuscripts of lesser importance) an additional clause is found in this verse. This clause has Cain saying, "Let us go out in the fields," and its inclusion certainly makes good sense. Accordingly, Genesis 4:8 in the *Good News Bible* reads: "Then Cain said to his brother Abel, 'Let's go out in the fields.' When they were out in the fields, Cain turned on his brother and killed him."

While the Septuagint is one of the most important supporting witnesses for the Hebrew text, it cannot always be trusted, for its translators often attempted to smooth over difficulties or to introduce what to them seemed to be greater consistency. In Genesis 48:15 the Hebrew text has "he blessed Joseph," speaking of the blessing pronounced by Jacob while his hands were on the heads of Ephraim and Manasseh (vv. 15–20). It was quite natural for the Septuagint, which was later followed by the Syriac, to substitute "the boys" for "Joseph," since Joseph is not mentioned in the blessing but the two boys are. But what the Septuagint translators overlooked was how a Hebrew father was looked upon as blessed in the blessing of his offspring, even as a son might be cursed in the cursing of his father. The latter is what occurred in the case of Ham and his son Canaan; the son was cursed for the evil action of the father (Gen. 9:22, 25–27).

In 1 Samuel 17:4 the Septuagint and also a Qumran manuscript give the height of Goliath as "four cubits and a span" (about six and a half feet) in place of the "six cubits and a span" (somewhat over nine feet) of the Massoretic text. Perhaps some early scribes felt that "nine cubits" was entirely too much, but "four cubits and a span" would hardly have qualified Goliath as a "giant" capable of using such heavy armor and weapons as the rest of the description indicates. The ancient Sudanese were fully six feet tall and probably more, but they were not regarded as giants. It seems better, therefore, to follow the Massoretic text in translating this verse.

Genesis 49 is a particularly difficult chapter textually. One clause of verse 26 does not seem to fit the context at all. After a long series of different kinds of blessings, ending with "the blessings of the breasts and of the womb," there is the statement from Jacob: "The blessings of thy father have prevailed above the blessings of my progenitors." Scholars have recognized that by a change of one letter, the transposition of another, and a shift in word division, this clause could be interpreted to read "blessings of grain and flowers." Such an alteration represents what is called technically a "conjecture" and identified in the *Good News Bible* as "probable text." In all such instances, however, the interpretation of the Massoretic Hebrew text is also given or described as "unclear."

In Psalm 74:14 *The New English Bible* has introduced a rather appealing conjecture, namely, "sharks" in place of the Hebrew "desert animals" or "desert peoples." In this passage about crushing the heads of the monster Leviathan, a legendary creature, probably mentioned in this context as a symbol of Egypt, a word meaning "sharks" seems to fit perfectly, and this meaning is made possible by only a slight change in the form of the Hebrew text. There are, nevertheless, a number of important reasons for retaining the Hebrew text. The allusion to the defeat of Egypt is probably linked also to the theme of the victory of the Israelites, who as the "desert peoples" are symbolically referred to as the "desert animals" who fed on Leviathan's body. Accordingly, the *Good News Bible* reads: "you crushed the heads of the monster Leviathan and fed his body to desert animals."

In some instances textual problems involve only the addition or omission of a single letter. In the case of "Danel" or "Daniel" in Ezekiel 14:14 and 28:3, the difference involves the smallest letter in the Hebrew alphabet. The normal form of the name of the prophet Daniel has the Hebrew letter *yod* (the small, apostrophe-sized mark), but the name of the person in the two passages of Ezekiel lacks this letter. Some scholars have argued that it would seem strange for Ezekiel to associate such a recent prophet as the Daniel of the exile with the ancient figures Noah and Job. They assume, therefore, that Ezekiel must have referred to some other ancient hero famous for his righteous life. No one can be certain of who really was being identified in Ezekiel, but it is only fair to the reader to indicate that the form of the name in Ezekiel is not identical with the name of the prophet.

In some instances textual differences arise because of the uncertainty as to whether a proper name is the name of a place or of a person. The same words are frequently used in both ways. In Hosea 6:7 there is an especially complex problem, for the Hebrew text reads literally "like Adam," in which case the phrase must be related to "breaking the covenant." But with a slight change in the form of the first letter, the meaning would be "at Adam," a reference to a place in Palestine. If the latter is the correct meaning, the phrase must be related to "entered the land." The translators of the King James Version understood this phrase in the sense of "like men," which is also possible, and *The New English Bible* introduces a further modification in the name, rendering it as "at Admah."

The translation committee for the *Good News Bible* found that two passages in the Hebrew were especially difficult in terms of text. The Song of Deborah (Judg. 5) has more than forty-five textual problems noted in Kittel's Hebrew text. Job 19:25–26 is a very short passage, and yet it is extremely complex; five of the seven words in verse 26 involve textual variants.

In some cases there seems to be simply no way in which a textual difficulty can be resolved. Just such a case is 1 Samuel 13:1. In Hebrew it reads, "Saul was years old when he became king, and he was a king of Israel for two years." The Revised Standard Version notes the two defected elements in this verse by using three dots: "Saul was . . . years old when he began to reign; and he reigned . . . and two years over Israel" and adds a footnote indicating that certain expressions of time have dropped out. The King James Version has a radical reinterpretation of the text: "Saul reigned one year; and when he had reigned two years over Israel," but this rendering is obviously the result of trying to make sense of a text which really doesn't make sense. In the *Good News Bible* the entire verse is placed in a footnote, with an indication that the Hebrew text is defective at two points. This seems much better than following any one of the more or less fanciful conjectures which have been suggested.

Despite all the textual problems which do exist in the Bible, what is really remarkable is the extent to which these ancient documents have been so faithfully and accurately copied and recopied through the centuries. A study of the problems alone would tend to give a wrong impression of the Scriptures as a whole. Considering how impossible it is to copy any long document with one-hundred percent accuracy, it is a high tribute to both the scholarship and devotion of ancient scribes that they have preserved for us such remarkably faithful copies of documents written and brought together over a period of more than a thousand years, and now for more than another thousand years known as a single corporate whole—the Bible.

CHAPTER TEN

Science Comes to the Aid
of Bible Translators

The science of semantics ("semantics" is just a technical term for "meaning"), which is only part of the even more inclusive and rapidly developing science of semiotics (the science of signs and symbols), has been providing us with totally new insights as to the real nature of translation. There was a time when people expected that any word in a source language should and could be represented by a corresponding word in a receptor language. Anything other than a straight word-for-word rendering was not considered to be translating at all—it was called "paraphrasing." But in Matthew 5:41 there is a Greek verb *angareuō*, which simply cannot be expressed by a single word in English because it has entirely too many highly specific features of meaning (called "components" in the science of semantics). For this verb even the translators of the King James Version used three English words, "compel . . . to go," yet these do not include all the meanings of *angareuō*. This one Greek verb combines at least the following specific components of meaning: (1) "burdensome activity," (2) "which is compelled," (3) "by officers or soldiers of occupation forces," and (4) "on noncitizens or persons without high status." Accordingly, when the *Good News Bible* has "if one of the occupation troops forces you to carry his pack one mile," it is only representing accurately the real meaning of the underlying Greek verb. Though the English requires nine words to say what is expressed in one word in Greek, this is not a paraphrase: it is a translation. To express any less than what is communicated by this translation in

Today's English Version would be to short-change the Greek text.

An even more important principle in the science of semantics is the requirement to recognize fully and accurately the diversity of meanings of single terms. The older idea that words represent "points of meaning" in the "geography of thought" has given way to a much more accurate scientific metaphor, namely, that the meanings of words are "territories of meaning." Not only so, but these "territories" often have highly irregular boundaries and frequently overlap with the semantic territories of other words. Some words have very large areas of meaning, for example, "matter," "object," "thing," "action," "event," and "person," while other words have very restricted areas of meaning, for example, "raccoon," "bluebird," "oak," "tuberculosis," and "dahlia." What is important for the translator is to recognize that though each language divides up experience into a kind of verbal map of so-called "conceptual territories," the map of one language cannot be superimposed on the map of any other language. Corresponding words in two different languages never have exactly the same meanings. That means that the Greek term *kurios* may be translated into English as "Lord," "sir," "master," or "owner," depending on the context; *kurios* does not mean simply "Lord," as some persons have supposed and as some dictionaries seem to imply. Similarly, the Greek term *sarks* does not mean simply "flesh," as some Greek dictionaries for beginners might suggest. As given in the Greek lexicon edited by Arndt and Gingrich, the meaning of *sarks* overlaps in part with the meaning of the English terms "body," "person," "human nature," "physical limitations," "human standards," "unregenerate state," and "sexual urge." To attempt to translate the Greek term *sarks* always and only by the English word "flesh" would result not only in misleading and confusing renderings, but it would violate certain of the basic principles of communication.

If translators are to resolve the problems of equivalance of meaning, it is not enough for them to work out a series of rules-of-thumb as general guides as to when and where to expand, cut, substitute, or rearrange. Communication processes are far too complex for any such listing of "do's and don't's." A far more intricate and integrated system must be employed, and this is to be found in the joint sciences of semantics and communication theory.

The key to translation theory is based on the fact that languages differ primarily in form and not in what they can communicate. It is not the "what" of content but the "how" of form that basically distinguishes one language from another. Greek *en oikō*, Spanish *en casa*, German *zu Hause*, French *chez (moi)*, and English *at home* all differ in form, but have essentially the same meaning.

If we symbolize the formal structures of the source language (the language from which one is translating) as a square of a particular size, we may conveniently conceive of the formal structure of the receptor language (the language into which one is translating) as being a circle containing essentially the same spatial area. The translation process consists essentially in the transfer of a given quantity of meaning (the respective areas) from one formal structure of language to another.

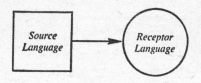

Figure 1.

Perhaps the best passage in the New Testament with which to demonstrate the implications of this principle of semantic equivalence and formal diversity is Mark 1:4, which in traditional translations reads in part, "John . . . preached the baptism of repentence unto the remission of sins." Unfortunately, most English-speaking persons do not know the word "remission," and so it is perhaps better to substitute "forgiveness." A series of nouns such as "baptism," "repentance," "forgiveness," and "sins" hung together only by prepositions is artificial even in English, and in many languages it is entirely impossible. In fact, in many languages there simply are no nouns for "baptism," "repentance," "forgiveness," or "sins," because these are really not objects but events, and events must be expressed by verbs, not by nouns. Furthermore, one cannot ordinarily speak of events in such languages without specifying who takes part in the events, the participants. In Mark 1:4, however, there are no indications in the immediate context as to who does what. In other words, the participants in the events of baptism, repentance, forgiveness, and sins are not indicated. Nevertheless, if this passage is to be really meaningful and natural, even in English, the participants need to be identified. But let us first identify some of the rather complex relations involved in this series of events. These can perhaps be best indicated by means of a diagram:

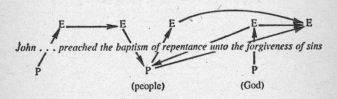

Figure 2.

The superimposed P's mark participants and the E's identify events. The parentheses around "people" and "God" indicate that these participants are not explicitly mentioned in the context, but they are fully implicit; the passage can only make sense if these implicit participants are included. An arrow from a participant to an event indicates that the participant is the actor in that event. An arrow leading from an event to a participant or to another event indicates that the second participant or event is the "goal" of the activity. The diagram of figure 2 indicates the following relations between the participants and the events:

John preaches (that which follows)
John baptizes the people
the people repent
God forgives the people
the people sin

This is not what the verse states, of course; it simply demonstrates the relations between participants and events which are implicit in the statement.

But determining the relations between the participants and events is only the beginning of a necessary analysis of such a complex text. One must also determine the meaning of the relation between the events involved. As indicated, the entire series of four events is the goal of the event indicated in the word "preached"; that is to say, the verbal nouns "baptism," "repentance," "forgiveness," and "sins" are a summary of the content of John's preaching. But what is the relationship between "baptism" and "repentance"? Some Greek grammars call this a "qualitative genitive construction," but that does not help much to explain the underlying significance. In reality, this noun sequence "baptism of repentance" is only a noun form of an underlying verb expression "repent and be baptized" (linguists often speak of the underlying structures as being the "deep structure" of an utterance). The "repentance" thus qualifies the "baptism" by being something which precedes it in time. The preposition "unto" points to purpose or result, and "sins" are the grammatical goal of the event of "forgiveness." In following out the implications of this type of analysis, Today's English Version has "John . . . preaching. 'Turn away from your sins and be baptized,' he told the people, 'and God will forgive your sins.' " The English text uses a few more words than the Greek text, and it requires certain rearrangements of order, but it does not contain any more meaning. It has only made explicit what is fully implicit in the immediate context of this verse.

Another way to understand what happens in the process of translating is to liken this process to what takes place when the contents of a wide-gauge freight train must be transferred to the cars of a narrow-gauge train. Obviously more cars are required in the second train and some of the objects which fit together into one large freight car must be redistributed in the cars of the narrow-gauge train. What is important in this process is not how the material is redistributed or even how many cars are required, but whether all the goods on the first train arrive at their destination on the second train. So it is with translating. What is important about the Greek verb *angareuō* in Matthew 5:41 and the series of nouns in Mark 1:4 is that the full meaning finally comes across in English translation.

In general the process of transfer from the source language to the receptor language requires the addition of words in order to communicate the same meaning. Good translations tend to be longer than their originals—but it does not follow that all longer translations are necessarily good ones. There are some instances, however, in which the translated message is actually shorter than the original. In the More language of West Africa, for example, a single verb is equivalent to "getting up early in the morning and going out to a desert place alone" (Mark 1:35). But whether there are more or fewer words in the translation than in the source text is not important. What is important is the extent to which the semantic components (that is, the distinctive features of the meaning in the source language) are properly represented in the receptor language. One might say that translators do not translate words but semantic components, since words are only the formal vehicle which carry the semantic content. To accomplish this result a certain amount of restructuring may be necessary. For example, in such a relatively simple expression as "he saw James the son of Zebedee, and John his brother" (KJV), there is a potential ambiguity for "his brother" could possibly mean the brother of Zebedee, and there is no clear indication that James and John were brothers. While the Greek text reflects the normal manner in which in New Testament times two sons of the same man would be identified, such an arrangement is not only confusing but even unnatural in English. Accordingly, an equivalent expression in English must undergo some restructuring: "he saw two brothers, James and John, the sons of Zebedee."

More extensive restructuring is required in John 1:13, which in the King James Version reads, "which were born, not of blood, nor of the will of the flesh, nor of the will of man, but of God." The problems of meaning in "blood" and "flesh" have already been discussed, but at this point the difficulties of syntax must also be taken into consideration. To begin a sentence with "which were born" and then to insert three negative contrasts, before coming to the contrastive conclusion, "but of God," poses real problems for the average reader, and especially for the average church congregation as it listens to the reading of this passage of Scripture. However, the relations of thought can be made quite clear and the meaning expressed much more accurately by a simple rearrangement of the components of meaning: "They did not become God's children by natural means, that is, by being born as the children of a human father; God himself was their father."

The process of Bible translation can be diagramed effectively by symbolizing the source as S, the form of the message as M, the receptors as R (figure 3). The squares and the subscripts, represent the source-language communication, and the circles with the subscripts, represent the communication in the receptor language. The difference in level represents the time span between the source and receptor languages, and the combined R and S symbolizes the dual role of the translator, who is a receptor of the biblical text but also the source for the form of the message in the receptor language.

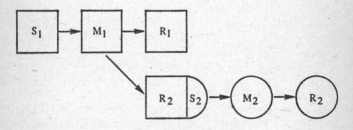

Figure 3.

This diagram, which is based on the fundamental model of communication, attempts to show graphically some of the major contrasts in roles and in formal structures; but it becomes even more instructive when one adds the typical role of the translation critic or assessor, the person who is generally called upon to determine whether a translation is satisfactory or not (figure 4).

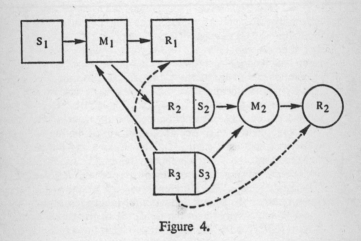

Figure 4.

The translation critic, identified as R_3 and S_3, normally compares the two texts (symbolized by solid line arrows) to determine if in his judgment the expressions contain accurate correspondences. The inherent difficulty in such a process is that the bilingual critic already knows the meaning of the source-language text, and he can recognize the meaning in the receptor text almost without regard to the problems which a monolingual receptor might have. In contrast with this traditional approach, the critic should investigate how typical receptors of the receptor text understand the message (indicated by broken lines). He could then compare this with how corresponding receptors understood the original message.

The fact that dictionaries may seem to justify certain correspondences in words is no proof that ordinary people will comprehend what is involved. For example, in a recent translation from French to English, *aspiration fugace* was rendered as "fugacious aspiration," easily justified on the basis of dictionary correspondences, but certainly not the way to represent the English phrase "fleeting breath." If the receptors for which a translation has been prepared do not actually understand a translation correctly, then it is not a correct translation, regardless of how one may be able to justify, by means of dictionaries or lexicons, the words used in the translation.

During World War II the United States Military issued an initial regulation on translation which required that "translations be sufficiently clear that anyone is likely to be able to understand." Even this regulation was found to be inadequate, and so it had to be revised to require that translations must be sufficiently clear "so that no one is likely to misunderstand."

In the case of one translation made for a tribe of Indians in North America, all the missionaries involved in the translation project agreed that a particular phrase in the Indian language would be quite suitable for "only begotten son," since the etymologies of the terms used in the phrase seemed to be perfectly clear. The Indians, however, all insisted that the expression was very unsuitable, for it would be understood by everyone as "only bastard child." Etymology means nothing in comparison with actual usage. It is the actual usage of an expression which must determine whether it can be used in a given situation. For example, an expression such as "goodbye" cannot be regarded as religious simply because it is historically derived from "God be with you."

Once a translator has determined the meaning of a passage, he must then decide how he can most accurately and effectively render it for his intended audience. Unfortunately, many translators never define their audience, and so they tend to translate with only themselves or their professional colleagues in mind. For the translators of the *Good News Bible* it was especially important to define the audience, for they had to employ words and grammar which would be appropriate to the "common language." To obtain some grasp as to what is

meant by "common language," the diagram in Figure 5 may
be of help.

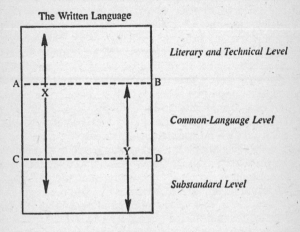

Figure 5.

Figure 5 is restricted to the written language and also to the
"consumer" role, that is, the language which people can read
and readily understand. X is a typical person on the educated
level, and Y an individual with relatively limited education. X
has a considerably wider range of reading ability and comprehension than Y, but he is not always able to read everything
on a literary or technical level, and similarly there may be a
number of substandard expressions which he does not readily
recognize or understand.

The line C–D marks a distinction between standard usage
and substandard usage, and in general a person such as X will
not employ forms below that line if he is writing for a general
or unknown audience. He may occasionally use such forms if
he is writing to intimate friends, but in communicating with
persons he does not know, substandard forms are normally
taboo for him. The line C–D is equally important for Y, for
though he often uses substandard forms himself (in fact, he

may not even be able to write in accordance with standard norms), he will not readily receive communications in substandard language if they come from persons or institutions on the level of X, for he would regard them as patronizing.

The rejection by Y of anything in the substandard range is well illustrated by the manner in which typical residents of Harlem in New York City rejected and even resented a translation of the Gospel of John which was produced in "Harlemese" English. Similarly, a group of young people in Norway refused to accept a translation of a Gospel which was prepared in their own "youth language." They not only felt that it was patronizing, but they insisted that by the time it was printed many of the idioms were already out of date.

The line A–B represents the top range of Y's consumer language, that is, the limits of his reading comprehension, and anything which is to be understood or accepted by Y must be within the common-language range.

This common-language range is also fully acceptable to X, at least for relevant messages. In reality this range is precisely where he communicates and receives communications most of the time. He may enjoy dipping into literary works now and then, but most of his reading, and certainly most of his writing, will be on the common-language level, where he is really most at home.

The common-language range is not, however, a narrow band of monotonous usage. It contains a relatively wide variety of forms, so that a common-language translation of the Gospel of Mark sounds different from the common-language translation of the Epistle to the Hebrews. Mark and the writer of Hebrews used widely differing literary styles when they wrote in Greek, and the differences are clearly carried over in a common-language translation. Likewise, the narrative style of Joshua is quite distinct from the poetry of Job and the Psalms, both in the original Hebrew and in common-language translation.

The rendering of poetry constitutes one of the most difficult of all problems in the preparation of a common-language translation. That is not merely because poetry is traditionally on a rather high literary level but also because the roles of poetry may differ appreciably from one language to another.

In the Hebrew Old Testament many of the discourses of the prophets are in poetic form, since it was customary in the ancient East to use poetry for important teachings and warnings. In present-day English, however, poetry is simply not used for such utterances. No English-speaking statesman would ever think of denouncing enemies in poetry or delivering an ultimatum in measured stanzas. For translators of the Bible the role of the content is actually more important than the correspondent formal structures. Accordingly, those prophetic passages which have a poetic content (for example, Isaiah 40—43, 53—55, Jeremiah 8:18—9:11, Ezekiel 19, Joel 1 and 2) are all rendered as poetry in the *Good News Bible*. But one cannot make poetry out of what is basically prose simply by chopping up the discourse into lines and employing various kinds of indentation. Furthermore, what may be dignified and effective prose can appear awkward if printed as poetry.

The basic concern of the translator, whether he is translating prose or poetry, is to reproduce the "closest natural equivalent" of the source-language text. He knows full well that he can never attain complete identity of meaning. That is impossible even within a single language, for no two persons ever mean exactly the same thing by the same utterance. Their use of language depends essentially upon their own experience, and the experience of no two persons is ever completely identical. Translators recognize, therefore, that in the use of words such as "salvation," "love," "grace," and "hell," it is impossible to communicate all and only what is implied in the source-language text. But they do aim to use expressions which are functionally equivalent, so that the reader may be able to understand and appreciate how the original receptors understood the message.

But mere "equivalence" is not enough; it must be the "closest," not just any possible equivalence. For example, in John 9:18 the Greek text reads literally, "but the Jews did not believe concerning him, that he had been blind" (speaking of the man who had been born blind and had been healed by Jesus). The English term "Jews" is a literal equivalent of the Greek word, but it is clear from the context that the passage does not refer to all Jews or even to Jews in general, but to the Jewish authorities. Accordingly, the *Good News Bible* renders this verse: "The Jewish authorities, however, were not willing to believe that he had been blind." In other places, too, where the Greek term for "Jews" really refers to the "Jewish authorities," the latter term is used.

An equivalence must also be "natural." In a sense, a Bible translation into English should seem as though the original account had been written in English and not in Greek or Hebrew. Even though the content of the message may seem strange or "new"—the fact that God loves people is always "news"!—nevertheless the verbal medium in which the message is communicated should not seem foreign, archaic, or contrived.

The criterion of "closest natural equivalence" is the touchstone of faithful translation—the guarantee of both accuracy and acceptability, a principle of communication in which form gives way to meaning and content has priority over structures.

CHAPTER ELEVEN

Good News Travels Fast

Scarcely had the New Testament in Today's English Version been published than people began to ask, "When are you going to translate *Good News for Modern Man* into French?" "Never!" was the surprising answer given by the Bible Societies. But of course—a translation in common language for one of the major world languages should never be made from a translation into another language, no matter how good that translation may be. A translation into French would have to be made directly from Greek and Hebrew by persons who are competent in those original languages but who also speak French as their own mother tongue.

A common-language translation into French had, in fact, already been started. It was started even before the Today's English New Testament was published. The translator, Jean-Claude Margot, a Swiss pastor of the Free Church, combines rare gifts of pastoral concern, sound biblical scholarship (he had already written a commentary on 1 Peter), and an unusually keen capacity to express the message of Scriptures in his mother tongue. When it was published, this common-language New Testament in French, called *Bonnes Nouvelles Aujourd'hui*, became an almost instant success, especially in French-speaking Africa, where Christian churches are flourishing.

Another major common-language translation has been made in Brazilian Portuguese. The work was done by a gifted committee consisting of a pastor who is a psychologist and specialist in biblical languages, a theologian who is president of a school for training lay leadership, and a woman who has specialized in working among youth and who is especially sensitive to matters of style. In addition, several consultants, including Dr. Robert Bratcher, who grew up in Brazil, have been able to provide important help in exegetical matters. When the New Testament *Na Linguagem de Hoje* ("In the Language of Today") was published, it proved so popular that work was begun at once on a similar type of translation for the Old Testament.

And so it has been in still other languages: Arabic, Bicol, Cebuano, Chinese, Dutch, Finnish, German, Haitian Creole, Hiligaynon, Iloko, Indonesian, Italian, Korean, Lingala, Malay, Malayalam, Marathi, Miskito, Norwegian, Pilipino, Swahili, Tamil, Thai, Vietnamese, Yoruba—and many more.

To give prospective translators the necessary training for the production of these special kinds of translations, translators institutes were organized. The first such institute was held in Bobo Djoulasso, in the Upper Volta, West Africa, where thirty-five translators met under rather primitive conditions in a primary school during a vacation period. Other institutes quickly followed, held in more than thirty countries, including Cameroun, East Germany, Ghana, India, Indonesia, Papua New Guinea, Peru, Philippines, Taiwan, Uganda, Zaire, and Zambia, and involving more than fifteen hundred translators working in well over two hundred different languages.

For major languages spoken by people in industrialized societies with large urban populations and highly diversified occupations and levels of education and training, common-language translations are essential. In such societies the common language serves as the common medium of communication in a heterogeneous society with its different levels of language use. But for smaller languages, spoken primarily in so-called face-to-face societies, where differences of occupation, languages, and training are minimal, a somewhat different though related type of translation may be employed. Called technically a "popular-language translation," this type of translation avoids the extremes of specialized jargon, as, for example, the esoteric language of the medicine men or of the native courts and taboo forms of speech. Such popular-language translations can exploit more fully the total range of language use because the languages are not divided into strata such as those illustrated in figure 5 on page 106. Popular-language translations have already been produced in such well-established languages as Yóruba, spoken by several million people in Nigeria, and in Ponapean, spoken by only sixteen thousand people in Micronesia, as well as in such a relatively new language as Haitian Creole, the native tongue of some six million people of Haiti.

In some circumstances, however, even a common-language translation is too difficult for certain people, and so selections for new readers must be prepared, based on a common-language translation but still further simplified for the sake of those who need some transitional reading matter. These literacy translations are not in the childish language of beginning primers, with such sentences as "Mary sees the cat" and "The cat sees Mary." The texts are valid translations, but they employ a level of language which is intelligible and manageable for all new readers, both adults and children. Compare, for example, three texts of Luke 8:11–15, first in the Revised Standard Version, then in the *Good News Bible,* and finally in *Selections for New Readers:*

Revised Standard Version

11 Now the parable is this: The seed is the word of God. 12 The ones along the path are those who have heard; then the devil comes and takes away the word from their hearts, that they may not believe and be saved. 13 And the ones on the rock are those who, when they hear the word, receive it with joy; but these have no root, they believe for a while and in time of temptation fall away. 14 And as for what fell among the thorns, they are those who hear, but as they go on their way they are choked by the cares and riches and pleasures of life, and their fruit does not mature. 15 And as for that in the good soil, they are those who, hearing the word, hold it fast in an honest and good heart, and bring forth fruit with patience.

Good News Bible

11 "This is what the parable means: the seed is the word of God. 12 The seeds that fell along the path stand

for those who hear; but the Devil comes and takes the
message away from their hearts in order to keep them
from believing and being saved. 13 The seeds that fell
on rocky ground stand for those who hear the message
and receive it gladly. But it does not sink deep into
them; they believe only for a while but when the time of
testing comes, they fall away. 14 The seeds that fell
among thorn bushes stand for those who hear; but the
worries and riches and pleasures of this life crowd in
and choke them, and their fruit never ripens. 15 The
seeds that fell in good soil stand for those who hear the
message and retain it in a good and obedient heart, and
they persist until they bear fruit.

Selections for New Readers
This is what the story means:
　　the seed is the word of God.
　　The seeds that fell along the path
　　　　stand for the people who hear.
　　　　But the Devil comes
　　　　　and takes the word
　　　　　　away from their hearts
　　　　　in order to keep them
　　　　　　from believing
　　　　　　and being saved.
The seeds that fell on rocky ground
　　stand for those who hear the word
　　　　and receive it gladly.
　　　　But it does not sink deep into them.
　　　　They believe only for a little while.
　　　　　But when the time of testing comes,
　　　　　　they give up.
The seeds that fell among weeds
　　stand for those who hear.
　　But they worry,
　　　　they think only about being rich,
　　　　and they just want to have a good time.
　　All this ruins them
　　　　and they never produce anything.
The seeds that fell into good ground
　　stand for those who hear the word
　　and keep it in a good and faithful heart.
　　　They last until they bear fruit.

The Word of life must become life for all people, but that is only possible if all can understand, and so various levels of language can and must be used to meet the needs of all in every condition of learning and in every circumstance of life.

The response of people to common-language and popular-language translations, as well as to selections for new readers, has been overwhelming, with more than a billion copies of Bibles, New Testaments, portions, and selections circulated by the Bible Societies within the last ten years in scores of languages throughout the world. These books, portions, and selections have not gone primarily into church pews so that Christians may read them on Sunday mornings. They have gone out to where people are. One supermarket chain in Alabama sold more than 8,000 copies of Today's English Version New Testament in a couple of months, and five supermarket chains in Great Britain sold over 200,000 copies in record time, displaying them at the checkout counter along with cigarettes and chewing gum.

At Michigan State University 32,000 copies were distributed one fall. One student read the title on the cover and exclaimed, "What good news can there possibly be for modern man?" But when he opened the book and saw that it was the New Testament, his reaction was, "That's what I want."

Good News for Modern Man has been a hit in the nation-wide Baseball Chapel program, the brainchild of Watson Spoelstra, a former sportswriter for the Detroit News. Spoelstra was deeply concerned that so few baseball players during season have a chance to attend church because of Sunday morning warm-ups for afternoon games. Baseball Chapels began with two teams in 1973, and by the end of 1975 twenty-four teams had joined and attendance was far greater than anyone had imagined could be possible. As Spoelstra noted, "This doesn't mean the players are pious or claim to be saints . . . but a lot of guys are checking things out . . . looking for answers."

Several hundred thousand people have found their *Good News for Modern Man* in the popular motor hotels known as Day's Inns, where special copies are printed with a cover which reads, "Take with You for Spiritual Uplift." In Wood

River, Illinois, as in hundreds of other communities, a men's club distributed 2,000 copies of the New Testament. The Grace Lutheran Church (Missouri Synod) in Vancouver, Washington, started out to distribute some 200 copies of *Good News,* but the demand grew so rapidly that within a few months they had placed more than 24,000 copies in the hands of people who eagerly received them.

Southern Baptist and Nazarene churches have had special editions printed so that they could be used in Bible study programs. The text of Today's English Version of the New Testament has been approved for use by Roman Catholics, first by Cardinal Cushing and later by Archbishop Whealon.

In a few churches some people were alarmed to think that people were being encouraged to read a text other than what had been used in the past. The Reformed Presbyterian Church appointed a commission to look into some of the queries and objections which had been voiced by certain members concerning this version. The report of this commission assured the constituency that Today's English Version "fulfills the requirement of the Westminster Confession of Faith," and went on to say, "it is erroneous to suppose that a translation must slavishly conform to the syntax, metaphors, and idioms of the Biblical text in order to be judged a faithful translation. . . . Today's English Version renders doctrinally significant passages with greater clarity and in some instances with greater faithfulness to the meaning of the Greek text than does the time-honored King James Version." Similar statements have been published in the *War Cry,* the official publication of the Salvation Army.

With *Good News for Modern Man* traveling so fast and being read by so many millions, it is no wonder that some people became somewhat fearful that this new translation would take the place of traditional texts. But there should have been no reason for worry. There is always a place and a need for traditional translations which respond to the concerns and reflect the backgrounds of millions who have grown accustomed to them and have been spiritually nurtured by them.

Some persons have been concerned that the very multiplicity of translations would in a sense destroy the authority of the

Bible, since differences of wording would seem to dilute the impact of the contents. But again, such fears have been proved unwarranted. Authority is never dependent upon verbal formulas, but upon people's understanding what is meant. Moreover, the more Bible translations there are, the more people will read them.

The last two decades have witnessed an amazing number of new translations of the Bible into English, but multiplicity of translations is not really something new. From the time of the King James Version in 1611 until the Revised Standard Version in 1952, more than five hundred different translations of at least one book of the Bible had been published in English. Furthermore, the vitality of the church is almost always directly proportionate to the number of translations being produced, in English as well as in other languages, and the extent to which these are distributed, especially to people outside the regular church constituencies.

Unfortunately, there are instances in which people actually prefer translations which they do not understand. An Indian in Guatemala once said, "Oh, I prefer the Bible in Spanish, rather than in my own language, which, of course, I can understand better. But in Spanish the words sound so beautiful—and I don't have to do anything about it." Sadly enough, that Guatemalan Indian is not the only person with such an attitude. There is no magic, however, in the words of the Scriptures; the power is in their message—perhaps too much power for some persons.

The day when people could boast of "one nation, one religion, and one Bible" is long since passed. Our world is increasingly cosmopolitan and each nation is more and more an aggregation of many different kinds of people with many different backgrounds and quite diverse needs. This is especially true of the United States with its great variety of ethnic and cultural entities and its rapidly growing biblical illiteracy, even within the so-called "Bible Belt." In such circumstances the *Good News Bible* can be of strategic importance in reaching out beyond church membership to those who have never been nurtured on traditional biblical terminology. Today's English Version is one of the most effective tools in evangel-

ism, directed both to those who have never become acquainted
with the time-hallowed religious vocabulary and to those who
have been alienated from established religious institutions.

This may be one reason why Today's English Version has
been so popular on university campuses and with persons
like Jim P. A graduate of a prestigious Ivy League school,
a rapidly rising tennis pro, and a man with an independent
income, he had everything coming his way. Or apparently
so—until one day he cracked up and was committed to an
institution. "I guess I was a hopeless case," Jim explained,
"destined to rot behind those narrow windows in that locked
ward. But one day in the TV room I noticed a paperback
with newspaper mastheads on it. I was just curious—and
believe me, I would never have picked up one of those black-
book Bibles, but this New Testament was different. I could
understand it, and when finally I discovered that God really
loved me—well, that changed everything, and within a few
months I was dismissed. I tell you, that's good news."

The *Good News Bible* can also be used effectively as a guide
to the meaning of the more traditional translations. Many
Bible study groups continue to use the King James Version as
their official text, but many of the participants in such groups
have found that Today's English Version is an indispensable
help in understanding precisely what the various passages actually mean.

One of the most meaningful methods of Bible study is to
undertake a comparison of different translations. The use of
four or five different translations inevitably leads to serious
discussion of what is meant and why. If the problem is one
of text, an examination of the footnotes can be very instructive, and this will almost inevitably lead participants to dig
deeper into the history of how our Bible came to us. Differences of interpretation force people to consult commentaries
and other background helps. But even without such diverse
texts and varied interpretations, discussions of different insights arising out of different translations can make the reading and studying of the Scriptures an exciting experience.

For group reading the *Good News Bible* is ideal, since the
vocabulary consists of well-known words and the grammar is

clear and plain. No one is embarrassed by encountering "impossible words," and there need be no gaps in sound as people mumble along through tortuous phrases.

For family devotions the *Good News Bible* can make all the difference in the world. As one boy put it, "That's for us, too." The same can apply to Sunday school teachers. Others may discover what one teacher found out after he had used *Good News for Modern Man* in order to understand the meaning of the passage. "I don't mind teaching," he said, "when I know what I'm talking about."

Discovering what it's all about is precisely the purpose of the Word of life, something which Rob McCarthy, popular Australian pop singer, experienced. As Rob described his life, "I had been on one great ego-trip . . . the drug scene, Eastern mysticism. . . . I had been deeply studying Hinduism in the hope of finding an answer to life's deepest questions. I began to read the Bible in Today's English in the hope of finding out just who this Jesus character was, but I was looking for my own version of Jesus, a kind of Hinduized guru or teacher who had seen the light. How wrong I was! By the time I had read the Gospels, God had blown my mind. There was no more philosophy and mythology here. Jesus was a real man in the real world of history and much more. He was God, and I knew it."

One copy of *Good News for Modern Man* was torn into many pieces, not in order to destroy it, but to share it. A friend went to visit a young black doing time in a state penitentiary and left with him a copy of the *Good News*. When the visitor returned a few weeks later, the young prisoner had only a few torn pages left. Questioned about it, he explained that when he had read some of the book to his cell mates, they each wanted some of it for themselves. The only thing to do was to tear the book apart and divide it among them. When this intense interest became known, twenty copies of the New Testament were obtained and distributed among the prisoners; but there was still demand for more. Then fifty New Testaments were asked for, later a hundred, and before long several hundred copies had been put into the hands of men who found not only something which they could read but something which really spoke to them. As one prisoner had once commented, "When I read that book, it read me."

Here lies the power of the Book of books—a message communicated by the Spirit of God to prophets and evangelists in ancient times and communicated by that same Spirit to men and women today. Their transformed lives witness to the way in which this message of life has been translated into their own lives.

Also available in Fount Paperbacks

A Historical Introduction to the New Testament
ROBERT GRANT

'This splendid book is a New Testament introduction with a difference . . . All students of the New Testament will welcome this original and courageous study.'
Professor James S. Stewart

The Historical Geography of the Holy Land
G. ADAM SMITH

'A classic which has fascinated and instructed generations of students. This masterpiece among the vast literature on the Bible . . . will continue to delight readers as well as to inform.'
H. H. Rowley

The Dead Sea Scrolls 1947-1969
EDMUND WILSON

'A lucid narrative of the discovery of the scrolls which soon turns into a learned detective story; then an account of the excitement, the consternation and the intrigues.'
V. S. Pritchett, New Statesman

The Gospels and the Jesus of History
XAVIER LEON-DUFOUR

'This book is far more than an introduction to the study of the Gospels. With its detailed study of the Gospels and of the other New Testament books it is an excellent introduction to the Christology of the New Testament.' *William Barclay*

Also available in Fount Paperbacks

The Divine Pity
GERALD VANN

Undoubtedly Gerald Vann's masterpiece. Many people have insisted that this book should not merely be read, but re-read constantly, for it becomes more valuable the more it is pondered upon.

The Founder of Christianity
C. H. DODD

A portrait of Jesus by the front-ranking New Testament scholar. 'A first-rate and fascinating book . . . this book is a theological event.' *Times Literary Supplement*

Science and Christian Belief
C. A. COULSON

'Professor Coulson's book is one of the most profound studies of the relationship of science and religion that has yet been published.' *Times Literary Supplement*

Something Beautiful for God
MALCOLM MUGGERIDGE

'For me, Mother Teresa of Calcutta embodies Christian love in action. Her face shines with the love of Christ on which her whole life is centred. *Something Beautiful for God* is about her and the religious order she has instituted.' *Malcolm Muggeridge*

Jesus Rediscovered
MALCOLM MUGGERIDGE

'. . . one of the most beautifully written, perverse, infuriating, enjoyable and moving books of the year.'
David L. Edwards, Church Times

Also available in Fount Paperbacks

A Historical Introduction to the New Testament
ROBERT GRANT

'This splendid book is a New Testament introduction with a difference. . . . All students of the New Testament will welcome this original and courageous study.'

Professor James S. Stewart

The Foundations of New Testament Christology
R. H. FULLER

'A most important book. . . . It is a most exciting book with a splendidly imaginative grasp of the way in which the gospel unfolded as it was planted in different soils . . . this book will remain a major contribution to Christological origins.'

New Christian

Our Experience of God
H. D. LEWIS

How do we know that religious assertions are true? There can hardly be a question of greater importance than this for religious studies. It is the question with which this book is mainly concerned, and in dealing with it the author also discusses other topics of current interest.

The Boundaries of Our Being
PAUL TILLICH

In this volume are collected together Tillich's magnificent series preached in Universities and colleges between 1947 and 1963 and previously published as two books. Also included is the autobiographical sketch *On the Boundary*.

Also available in Fount Paperbacks

The Founder of Christianity
C. H. DODD

'A first-rate and fascinating book . . . This book is a theological event. It is to be unreservedly recommended and may play a powerful part in the revival of a positive and intelligent Christianity.' *Times Literary Supplement*

The Plain Man Looks at the Bible
WILLIAM NEIL

This book is meant for the plain man who would like to know what to think about the Bible today. It deals with the relevance of the Bible and restates its message for the twentieth century.

The Bible Story
WILLIAM NEIL

'A real spiritual experience . . . written in an easy and readable style that makes it difficult to put the book down. I can think of no better way of interesting anyone in reading the Bible than by putting this book into his hands.'
R. C. Fuller, Scripture Bulletin

Companion to the Good News
J. RHYMER AND A. BULLEN

'The book admirably sums up what a beginner needs to know about the background and content of the New Testament and states the critical problems fairly.'

The First Christmas
H. J. RICHARDS

'Many readers will be grateful for a Biblical scholarship which gives a fresh relevance to these beautiful passages of Scripture.'
Expository Times